101
Creative Strategies for Reaching Unmotivated Student Learners

A practical resource
of approaches and
activities for helping
unmotivated, discouraged
and/or disruptive students
(grades 2-8)

Susan J. Smith-Rex, Ed.D and James H. Rex, Ph.D.

© 2005 by YouthLight, Inc.
Chapin, SC 29036

Layout and design by Tonya Daugherty
Edited by Susan Bowman

ISBN—1-889636-69-X

Library of Congress
Control Number:
2004112334

10 9 8 7 6 5 4 3 2 1
Printed in the United States

PO Box 115 • Chapin, SC 29036
(800) 209-9774 • (803) 345-1070 • Fax (803) 345-0888
yl@sc.rr.com • www.youthlight.com

We gratefully acknowledge the insights and knowledge gained from past collaboration with our friends and collegues and, most especially, from Kim "Tip" Frank, Ed.S. LPC and Teresea A. Mathis, Ed.S.

About the Authors

Sue Smith-Rex, Ed.D. and James H. Rex, Ph.D. recently retired with a combination of sixty-five years in both higher education and K-12 education. Sue recently retired as a professor of Special Education from Winthrop University in Rock Hill, South Carolina. After thirty years of teaching in both public schools and higher education, she is now doing consulting work involving "at risk" issues and is the owner of a small business. In addition to co-authoring eleven books, she has conducted workshops throughout the United States on the topics of attention deficit hyperactivity disorder and school bullying. She has been the recipient of many professional awards: 1998- South Carolina Association of Counselors' Humanitarian Award; 1992-President Bush's Point of Light Award; and the 1988- Jefferson Pilot recipient of the Jefferson Award for public service.

Jim recently retired as president of Columbia College in Columbia, South Carolina. Prior to that he was the Vice President for Institutional Advancement at the University of South Carolina, the Vice Chancellor for Academic Affairs at Coastal Carolina University, and the Dean of Education at Winthrop University and at Coastal Carolina University. Jim was also on the faculty of the University of Toledo and taught high school English and coached varsity football in Ohio.

Sue and Jim remain committed to the improvement of teaching and learning for every student in America's schools and to the unique contribution our schools continue to make to the American Dream of equal opportunity for all. The Rexes have four adult children: Jeffrey, Adam, Siri, and Nathan.

Table of Contents

Overview

Our society places a high premium on motivation. Athletics, business, politics, education, self-improvement, and romance are only some of the areas where outstanding achievement is often attributed to high motivation. The star athlete, the recognized entrepreneur, the triumphant candidate, the high achieving student, the slimmed-down dieter, and the satiated suitor more often-than-not attribute their accomplishments to their drive to succeed—their motivation.

If you are reading this overview "something" or "someone" motivated you to purchase this book, or at least to pick it up and open the cover. That dynamic, that constellation of influences, that determines whether we decide to move from thought to action, from opportunity to effort, is the subject of uncountable exchanges—written and unwritten—between human beings over the centuries. Motivational discourse has been written, spoken, and sung by poets, dictators, artists, coaches, pastors, parents, teachers and countless others in an effort to move individuals or groups towards some type of behavioral outcome.

The genesis of a person's motivation may be positive, neutral, or negative. We may want to help others, or improve a situation. We may simply want to be recognized or appreciated. Or, we may want revenge or the satisfaction of watching someone fail or be humiliated. We all seem to know intuitively that some people are motivated for the "right" reasons and others for the "wrong" reasons. Certainly a Hitler or an Osama Bin Laden are examples of highly motivated individuals, but the genesis of their motivation and the horrors of the manifestation of their persistence and drive are hard lessons to the world of the dangers of misdirected motivation.

Introduction

Classroom Motivation and
Implications for Practice

Happily, most efforts to motivate others and ourselves are for constructive and productive reasons. And, nowhere is this more true than in the classrooms of America. Just as we have discarded the antiquated notion that only some children are capable of learning, we are also now realizing that all children are capable of being motivated to bring about that learning. While it is true that some children really do seem to be "born" highly motivated to learn about virtually everything in the world around them, most of the rest of us need some assistance in this area. Providing that assistance, successfully, is what this book is all about.

I. The Big Picture

Classrooms, laboratories, libraries, media centers, vocational shops, cafeterias, and athletic fields are some of the "arenas of learning" where motivation plays a role. In America's schools the students have appropriately been the primary subject of research into motivation, but let us not forget that teachers, administrators and even parents must also be remembered as we look at how motivation affects learning behavior and its outcomes. Teachers, administrators, and parents must, themselves, be motivated to optimize the learning environment in our schools. Legislation, financial support, the physical environment, the community's level of interest in its schools all play a role in how highly motivated the key adult players are in their efforts to help children learn.

Before we focus on the individual classroom and the teacher in that classroom, a few words need to be directed to one of the external factors affecting our schools and the motivation levels of those who work, learn and depend upon them. In a research study published in February of 2003 entitled, "The Effects of High-Stakes Testing on Student Motivation and Learning", Audrey Amrein and David Berliner asked if high-stakes testing policies lead to increased student motivation to learn? And, do these policies lead to increased student learning? After reviewing eighteen states' data and analyzing four independent achievement measures, the answer to both questions was, no. In fact, this study concluded that the use of high-stakes tests (eg. for granting diplomas, advancement to grade levels, rating schools, etc.) actually decrease student motivation and increase the proportion of students who leave school early. At a time when the No Child Left Behind Act of 2001 strives to make high-stakes testing even more pervasive nation-wide, this report, funded by the Rockefeller Foundation, makes one pause. Testing, done appropriately, and for the right reasons, is undoubtedly a useful tool and can be a motivational strategy. But when done poorly, and for the wrong reasons, it can actually hurt educational efforts. As we think about testing policies, we should remember the wisdom in the farmer's comment that weighing a pig every day won't ever make the pig any fatter. Eventually, you have to feed the pig.

II. What Teachers Think

Julian Elliot looked at what teachers believed about student motivation in the United States, United Kingdom and Russia (2003). Across all these cultures, teachers agreed upon the positive effects of: teacher-student relations; symbolic and material rewards; grades and marks; parental interest and involvement; partnerships with parents; and, success in learning. Apparently most teachers do believe that they, and others, can have a positive effect upon student motivation levels. How, then, do we act upon these beliefs? What does research say that can help provide directions to our effort?

III. Motivation and the Classroom

Teacher behaviors matter. They matter to students (Felner, Aber, Primavera, & Cauce, 1985; Goodenow, 1993; Wentzel & Asher, 1995); and, they matter to the academic achievement and social adjustment of students (Cohen & Wills, 1985; Noblit, 1993). Wentzel (1996) found that when perceived support from parents, peers, and teachers is considered jointly, perceived support from teachers has the most direct link to students' interest in school.

So, we know that students notice and care (even though many would rarely admit to this) about how teachers interact with them and their peers. We also know that while parents and peers may have significant effects on a child's motivational level, the teachers' behaviors and relationships with the student are the most important determinants of classroom interest and success.

Most of us know intuitively and/or from personal experience that most human beings will put forth their best efforts in a supportive environment that may include a boss, a coach, or a teacher whom they respect and whom they believe has their best interests at heart. According to Noddings (1992), the academic objectives of schools cannot be met unless teachers provide students with a caring and supportive classroom environment. And, while human behavior is far too complex to say that one variable will always have a specific effect, the research in this area provides strong evidence that students are more likely to engage in classroom activities if they feel supported and valued (Wentzel,1997).

What makes students feel valued? Students' descriptions of teachers who care and do not care provide some insight. Teachers who care were described as demonstrating democratic interaction styles, developing expectations for student behavior in light of individual differences, modeling a "caring" attitude toward their own work, and providing constructive feedback (Wentzel,1997).

While the research indicates that a caring and supportive teacher is important to successfully motivate students, it is not enough. It is necessary, but not sufficient. Other research has shown the equal importance of teaching and instruction. For example, researchers have documented significant relationships between classroom reward structures (Ames & Ames,1984), classroom organization (eg., Rosenholte & Wilson,1980; Slavin,1987), and the curriculum (eg., Renninger, Hidi, & Krapp,1992) on the one hand, and student motivation and academic work on the other. Apparently, teachers must not only be perceived as caring and supportive, but they must also be perceived as knowledgable, confident, creative and adaptive. Some might also want to add that they should be, "faster than a speeding bullet and able to leap tall buildings in a single bound", but as yet, there is no research to support this!

The following sections of this book, "101 Creative Strategies", are an attempt to keep the effort of reaching and motivating the unmotivated student from becoming a "superhuman" effort. The strategies are objective, descriptive, and to the point. They do not require significant resources or atypical classroom settings. Best of all, they are adaptable to almost any 2-8 grade level setting (and, often, beyond).

A last word before you begin to read about and utilize these strategies. Depending upon your personality, the history you have (if it is not the beginning of a new school year) with your students, and your teaching "habits" you will find some of them easier to attempt than others. That's fine. You may want to try the easier ones first. However, we caution you against being too comfortable in your efforts. Just as trying new foods often leads to new found favorites and even nutritional benefits, "stretching" yourself professionally and personally can be renewing in your increased sense of accomplishment.

Finally, if you decide to use this book as a teacher, a parent, a counselor, or other concerned professional, to help children find and enhance that essential element for their success called motivation, thank you. Thank you for your motivation to help them, and all of us!

Section 1

Healthy Student Self-Esteem

Strategy 1

Structuring the School to Create Greater Motivation for Students

There are many factors leading to poor motivation among students. Among the most common factors are the following:

Student:

- Immature
- Behavior problems
- Few friends
- Bored
- Low self esteem
- Fear of failure
- Poor study skills
- Few if any long term goals
- Angry
- Believing it's "cool" to fail

School:

- Impossible standards
- Low expectations
- Teachers who are too strict
- Lack of teacher patience
- Dull curricula
- Inflexible schedules
- Too much drill and practice
- Few after school clubs
- Curricular content is not gender friendly

Home:

- Lack of emotional support
- Parental job pressures
- Marital discord
- Financial concerns
- Little or no family time
- Education is not discussed
- Low expectations

The Learning Crisis for Many Boys!

The vast majority of underachieving school students are boys. Educators must be concerned with the crisis our schools are facing with the unmotivated male population. According to Dr. William Pollack's research from his book, *Real Boys*:

- They earn 70% of the D's and F's that teachers dole out.
- They make up two thirds of the students labeled "learning disabled".
- They make up 80% of the school dropouts.
- By the year 2007, out of every three college students two will be girls.

Girls outnumber boys in student government, honor societies, school newspapers, and debating clubs. Girls feel closer to their families, have higher aspirations and stronger assertiveness skills.

According to the 1997 report "Protecting Adolescents from Harm", the largest major factor protecting young people from emotional distress, drug abuse, and violence (other than closeness to the family) is school connectedness. Boys can thrive at school if there is a pervasive sense that they are:

- Welcomed
- Liked
- Accepted for who they are
  and how they enjoy learning

Since the majority of our teachers are females, they tend to teach the way girls learn best. Boys, however, prefer doing concrete, action oriented tasks. They are better kinesthetic learners and they perform better when given subject matter that relates to their interests. Listed are 10 ideas for schools to consider when motivating boys.

1. Be boy friendly when selecting subject matter.

2. Use teaching methods that work well for boys.

3. Respect the learning pace of every child.

4. Hire more male teachers!

5. Set up mentoring programs.

6. Increase the options for after school clubs.

7. Share with students Gardner's Multiple Intelligence Theory.

8. "Bully proof your school!"

9. Keep class size manageable.

10. Individualize and connect with students. Teach students not to procrastinate, how to use organizational tools, and how to self-monitor their efforts.

For more information about boys read:

Real Boys Workbook by William Pollack. Outlines "Some Do's and Don'ts with Boys." Also gives specific tips for talking to sensitive sons.

Speaking of Boys by Michael Thompson. Raising Cain coauthor answers "the most asked questions about raising sons", delving into topics such as male puberty and underage drinking.

The Men They Will Become by Eli Newberger. A thoughtful look at the emotional tug-of-war within boys.

A few books about girls to read is:

Queen Bees & Wannabes by Rosalind Wiseman. A book to help daughters survive cliques, gossip, boyfriends and other realities of adolescence.

200 Ways to Raise Girls' Self-Esteem by Will Glennon. Provides suggestions for boosting girls' confidence and strengthening self-image.

A book comparing boys and girls is:

Boys and Girls Learn Differently! by Michael Gurian. The latest on boys' and girls' thinking styles.

Strategy 2

Healthy Self-Esteems

By definition self-esteem refers to satisfaction with oneself. Having a healthy self-esteem places a student in a much less vulnerable position to dislike school and to have difficulty setting short-term or long-term goals. Individuals with a healthy self-esteem often have a feeling of peace and well-being. These are individuals who are more able to make better choices, be true friends, and demonstrate positive leadership skills.

According to educational literature from the American Medical Association, there are five important components to a healthy self-esteem:

1. A feeling of security (at home, school, and neighborhood).

2. A positive identity (feeling noticed for one's strengths and for doing what is expected).

3. A feeling of belonging (emotional goals have been identified).

4. A sense of purpose (meaningful goals have been identified).

5. A feeling of competence (being good at something one enjoys).

Based on these five components, ask designated students to complete the following questionnaire on page 17. For younger children the interviewer should ask the questions and write down the answers. This information should be shared with parents and become the core from which to build an intervention program. Information from the questionnaire will provide adults with insight as to how the student's self-esteem is developing.

Intervention Questionnaire

Name _____ Grade _____ Date_____

1. A feeling of security:

List people who love and support you.

1. _____

2. _____

5. _____

3. _____

4. _____

2. A positive identity:

List 3 of your greatest strengths.

1. _____

2. _____

3. _____

3. A feeling of belonging:

List 3 things you enjoy doing:

At Home: &   At School:

1. _____ _____

2. _____ _____

3. _____ _____

4. A sense of purpose:

List 3 things you hope to achieve at school this week. (short-term goals)

1. _____

2. _____

3. _____

List 3 things you hope to achieve at school this year. (long-term goals)

1. _____

2. _____

3. _____

5. A feeling of competence:

List 3 things you do well at school.

1. _____

2. _____

3. _____

Strategy 3

Student Questionnaire

It is important for teachers, counselors, and parents to better understand their children's attitudes. Questionnaires are helpful tools to assist adults and children themselves to find out what they like about school and what could make it better.

Two questionnaires follow. One is for elementary children and one is for middle/ high school students. Make two copies of the selected questionnaire for each student. This will allow both a "pre" and "post" program evaluation.

For nonreaders, the adult should read the questions. Inform the students that it is not a test. There are no right or wrong answers. Ask children to be honest and answer the questions in a way that shows how they really feel.

...stionnaire

your answer to each question.

to school: (Place an "X" on the correct feeling.)

I like it a lot.	...it.	OK	I don't like it very much	I don't like it at all.

	most of the time	sometimes	almost never
4. I like the students in my school:	❏	❏	❏
5. I feel bored in school:	❏	❏	❏
6. I get along with my classmates:	❏	❏	❏
7. I get along with my teacher:	❏	❏	❏
8. I get along with my family:	❏	❏	❏
9. I feel sad in my school:	❏	❏	❏
10. I feel angry in my school:	❏	❏	❏

	Good	OK	Poor
11. How do I rate myself as a friend?	❏	❏	❏
12. How do I rate myself as a leader?	❏	❏	❏
13. How do I rate my desire to get good grades?	❏	❏	❏
14. How do I rate myself at doing my homework?	❏	❏	❏
15. How do I rate my ability to use time wisely?	❏	❏	❏
16. How do I rate myself at asking for help when I need it?	❏	❏	❏
17. How do I rate myself at making good decisions my family would be proud of?	❏	❏	❏
18. How do I rate my ability to control my anger?	❏	❏	❏

Middle School/High School Attitude Questionnaire

Circle 1 to 5 when answering
the following 20 questions.

1 = poor

2 = ok

3 = good

4 = strong

5 = very strong

1. How do I get along with my classmates?
    1   2   3   4   5

2. How do I get along with my teachers?
    1   2   3   4   5

3. How do I get along with my family?
    1   2   3   4   5

4. How do I rate myself as a friend?
    1   2   3   4   5

5. How good am I at making new friends?
    1   2   3   4   5

6. How do I rate my physical fitness?
    1   2   3   4   5

7. How do I rate the tone of my voice?
    1   2   3   4   5

8. How do I rate the appeal of my smile?
    1   2   3   4   5

9. How do I best describe my maturity?
    1   2   3   4   5

10. How do I rate my ability to chat with
    people I don't know well?
    1   2   3   4   5

11. How do I rate my ability to make choices
    my family would be proud of?
    1   2   3   4   5

12. How do I rate my ability to set goals?
    1   2   3   4   5

13. How do I rate my leadership skills?
    1   2   3   4   5

14. How do I rate my respectful attitude?
    1   2   3   4   5

15. How do I rate my compassion for students
    who are being bullied at school?
    1   2   3   4   5

16. How do I rate my ability to say no to sex?
    1   2   3   4   5

17. How do I rate my ability to control my anger?
    1   2   3   4   5

18. How do I rate my ability to use time wisely
    each day?
    1   2   3   4   5

19. How do I rate my desire to get the best
    grades I can?
    1   2   3   4   5

20. How do I rate my future as an adult who
    will reach their potential?
    1   2   3   4   5

Comments:

_____

_____

_____

_____

_____

_____

Name _____

Grade _____

Girl ☐   or   Boy ☐

University, has done extensive research on the theory of multiple intelligences. Dr. Gardner theorizes that there are eight important types of intelligence, as outlined below.

The reason it is important for students, parents, and educators to support the Gardner Theory is that a strong self-esteem is largely based on the belief that all individuals are talented and valued in some area of their intellectual being (Gardner, 1983).

Multiple Intelligences

Make an overlay of the illustration below and discuss the varied intelligences with the students. Emphasize that the older an individual becomes the more intrapersonal and interpersonal intelligences stand out as the most important.

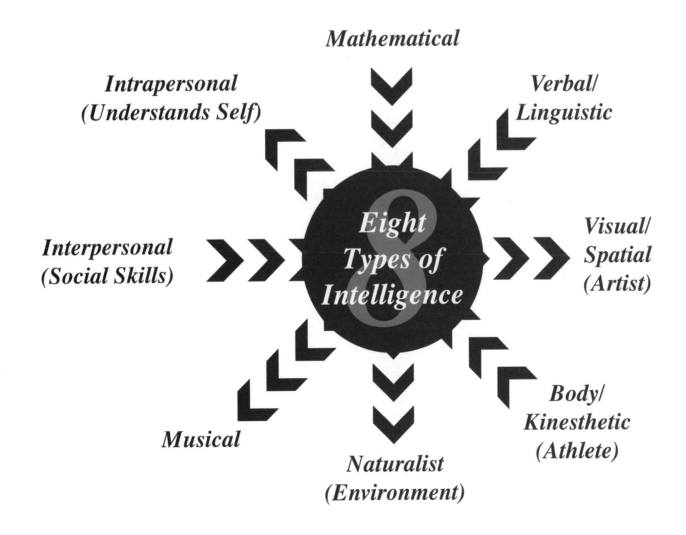

Strategy 5

The Totem Pole of Intelligences

Using the totem pole on this page, list the 8 types of intelligences on the pole. Begin with your strongest intelligence, or best way you learn, at the top and put the others in order from strongest to weakest down the pole. It is important to know and celebrate your greatest strengths. Everyone is talented in some ways. Discuss possible professions, hobbies and opportunities for each intelligence.

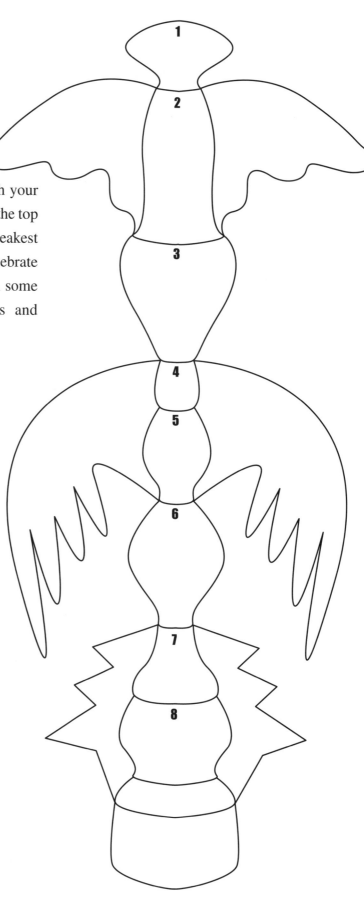

When it comes to feelings, people have positive/pleasant feelings and they have negative/unpleasant feelings. Everyone experiences both types during life but it is important to recognize the different types and not get "stuck" on unpleasant feelings for long periods of time.

Below is a list of examples of both types of feelings.

Pleasant Feelings	Unpleasant Feelings
(Feelings that usually help people succeed)	*(Feelings that make life more difficult)*
A. happy ____	G. sad ____
B. excited ____	H. mad ____
C. loved ____	I. frustrated ____
D. hopeful ____	J. disappointed ____
E. confident ____	K. embarrassed ____
F. organized ____	L. worried ____

Recognizing or knowing what feelings you have is very important. Throughout each day, stop for a minute and listen to your feelings. Ask, how am I feeling right now? Your body and mind will tell you.

Chart Your Feelings!

For one entire week, using the chart below, take a minute in the morning, after school, and before bed to identify your strongest feeling. Pick a feeling word from the list of pleasant and unpleasant feelings and put the letter in the appropriate box. At the end of the week, add up how often each letter or feeling occurred. By charting your feelings you get to know your own personality better, and you know which emotions you need to concentrate on improving.

Chart Your Feelings

Time	Monday	Tuesday	Wednesday	Thursday	Friday	Saturday	Sunday
Morning							
Afternoon							
Evening							

- Write the letter of your strongest feeling three times a day for one week.

- Add up how often each feeling occurred and place the total in the blank space above.

- Which feelings occur most often? _____

Adapted from Frank, T. and Smith-Rex, S. (1995). *Getting a life of your own*. Minn. MN: Educational Media.

Strategy 7

Negative VS Positive Thinking

Negative thinking, no matter what age, is a destructive waste of energy. The person who gets "stuck" in a cycle of negative thinking will often show some of the following signs:

1. You have more headaches than normal.
2. Your stomach or throat feels tied up like a knot.
3. You can't sleep well or you sleep too much.
4. You lose or gain too much weight.
5. You can't concentrate in school.
6. You seem to have little interest in most activities.
7. You have low energy levels.
8. You think about hurting others.
9. You feel worthless or guilty.
10. You have suicidal thoughts.
11. You retreat into your own world, not wanting to be around others.
12. You say things and do things you don't really mean.

Positive thinking is so important to one's good health and happiness. It allows us to set goals and gives us hope that our efforts will pay off.

Sometimes it can be very helpful to get out a piece of paper and make a list of everything that is worrying you. Using the "Front Burner—Back Burner" worksheet below, write the things from your list you really have no control of on the back burner. Write those items you have control over on the front burner. This activity is helpful to remove guilt over not fixing the back burner items and gives you permission to focus on the front burner.

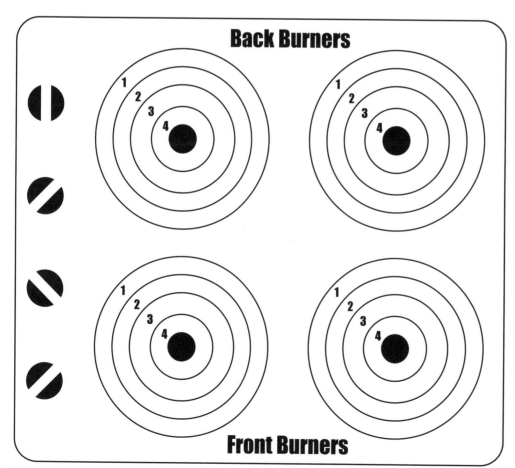

Adapted from Frank, T. and Smith-Rex, S. (1996). *Getting over the blues*. Minn.MN: Educational Media.

Who Has The Control?

Another strategy, which can help clarify to children which behaviors and/or responsibilities they have control over, is to read the following list and place each number inside or outside the body outline on this page.

Listed below are 15 words or phrases concerning getting along with people. Some of the words represent behaviors of which you have control. Write those numbers inside the body outline. For the behavior words of which you do not have control, write those numbers outside the body outline.

1. Attending school regularly

2. Crime in the neighborhood

3. Who your friends are

4. Good personal hygiene

5. Student attitudes

6. Being punctual

7. Following the school dress code

8. The school you attend

9. Good eye contact

10. Grades

11. A friendly smile

12. Hurtful behaviors by others

13. Family divorce

14. Giving compliments

15. A friend shoplifting

Remember, the only person who you can control is yourself. It is impossible to change others, but you can always strive to be the best you can be. Keep working on yourself and you will find that good friendships and school success will follow.

Strategy 9

Childish or Mature!

Using this flow chart, discuss with the students the fact that each hour of each day they have the choice to act childish or mature. Childish behavior is when you laugh inappropriately, draw negative attention to oneself, and/or interfere or prevent teaching and learning from occurring. Mature behavior is when students display considerate actions. In order to act maturely, one must have self-control. If students consistently display mature self-control, then others will respect them and they will respect themselves. Ultimately these qualities lead to success in students' personal and professional lives. Review the flow chart on a consistent basis in order for the students to visually memorize it.

Childish or MATURE

Self-Control

Respect

SUCCESS

Popular Mannerisms

Mannerisms are behaviors people do that can become habits. Those mannerisms that are perceived as positive or popular can become life-long mannerisms with practice and discipline. The mannerisms perceived as negative or bad (listed below) should be eliminated by using self-monitoring tools. (Examples of self-monitoring tools are on pages: 42-49.)

Some children have mannerisms that tell others they are happy, likeable and deserving students. Listed below are some of the positive mannerisms that make these children more accepted, respected, and successful.

Discuss these traits and then have each student rate themselves on the following scale.

Positive Mannerisms

1. Smile a lot

2. Use positive self-talk and affirmations

3. Do not act jealous of fellow classmates who are doing well. You can do it too!!

4. Say nice things about other people.

5. Use your support team to talk about important issues.

6. Reach out to help other people.

7. Remember that things on your back burners are out of your control. Focus your energy on things listed on your front burners.

8. Do what is expected of you on time and without complaining!

Types of People with Bad Manners

1. Hogs—People who don't know how to share and take turns.

2. Whiners—People that whine and complain when they don't get their way.

3. Big Mouths—People who can't shut up. They constantly talk, usually about themselves or other people.

4. Gross Outs—People who burp, pass gas around others, talk with a mouth full of food, or sneeze and cough without covering their mouth.

5. All Hands People—People who push, poke, and touch people when they shouldn't be.

6. Butinskys—People who constantly interrupt others and blurt out.

7. The Wrecking Crew—People who wreck other people's property.

Rate Your Popular Mannerisms

Place an "X" in the box that best describes you.

Name _____

	Strong	OK	Poor
I smile a lot.	❏	❏	❏
I do a lot of positive self talk	❏	❏	❏
I say nice things about others.	❏	❏	❏
I use my support team.	❏	❏	❏
I help other people often.	❏	❏	❏
I focus on things I need to do. (front burners)	❏	❏	❏
I do assignments on time without complaining.	❏	❏	❏
I have good manners when I eat.	❏	❏	❏

Strategy 11

Eye Contact and Handshakes

As students' attitudes about school learning improve, usually self-esteem improves as well. Others will view students as being more mature if they learn to look people in the eyes when they talk to them and to provide a firm handshake.

1. Look at a person's eyes.

2. Look at their eye color.

3. Count 1 – 2 then look away.

1. Handshakes can be too hard, too soft, or "just right."

2. Find the moderate level for a handshake.

3. Use your right hand.

4. Shake once, twice, and then release.

Strategy 12

Think and Look Assertive

Being assertive is a wonderful personal quality to have. It means that a person can act confident and let others know their true feelings in respectful, unhurtful ways. In order to be assertive a person must think and look assertive. Review with your students the following information and encourage students to take time each day to reinforce their personal beliefs and skills.

To THINK assertively a person must use positive self-talk. Practice statements such as:

I am capable.

I am respected.

I try to make mature choices.

I am aware of possible dangerous situations.

I know when to walk away from hurtful situations quickly.

I practice using an assertive tone with statements I may need to use such as:
   "Why are you acting childish?"
   "We both have the right to our own beliefs."

To LOOK assertive it is important that students practice sending out positive body language.

Keep your head up.

Walk like you have somewhere to go.

Stay calm.

Speak up.

Look at the person you are addressing.

Strategy 13

School Fears!

A strong, healthy self-esteem is based on feeling accepted. Fears can stand in the way of liking oneself, enjoying life, or reaching one's potential. Some of the fears that children often name that are associated with school are:

1. Speaking in front of class

2. Taking tests

3. Getting bad grades

4. Bullying

5. Trying new things

6. Changing schools

7. Not being liked by others

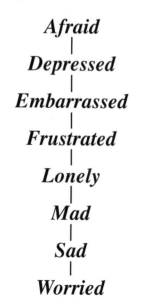

Personal fears can vary along a continuum from:

Afraid
|
Depressed
|
Embarrassed
|
Frustrated
|
Lonely
|
Mad
|
Sad
|
Worried

Children can accommodate a fear by avoiding school, putting forth effort in school, or learning to confront the fear. Being afraid over time can cause people to think or feel differently. A person may:

1. Have little interest in most school activities;

2. Have difficulty concentrating;

3. Have a low energy level; and

4. Say or do things that he/she doesn't mean.

Children may develop defenses, or walls, to hide their true feeling by: joking, daydreaming, talking-back, blaming, silence, or by displaying eating or sleep disorders.

It is very important for adults to help children learn how to focus on thinking "clear messages" vs. "muddy messages" about oneself. It will give children more confidence to overcome their school fears. Adults, through individual sessions, can help children identify behavioral defenses that have become negative habits. Refer to, and utilize, the information received through using the following strategies:

Help children to:

1. Identify any school fears;

2. Name defenses that have been used; and

3. List clear messages about themselves that will put them in a good mental position to make self-monitoring a useful intervention tool.

Strategy 14

Compliments and Everyday Statements

Underachievers may actually be academically unmotivated because of not feeling comfortable in school with their peers. Making friends and keeping friends is an ongoing "work in progress."

One of the hardest things for young people to do is to use positive comments, versus silly, immature "put-downs" with their peers. When a person sends clear messages to others, through a compliment or an appropriate everyday statement, they greatly increase their chances of being respected and well liked.

A compliment is when you say something nice to someone, such as: "I like your tennis shoes" or "You are a nice person." Compliments vary according to the gender, age, and the maturity of the student. Encourage students to give out compliments every day. Speaking clearly, smiling, and good eye contact supports the sincerity of the compliment.

An everyday statement is a sentence about almost anything, such as: "Where do you live?" or "Do you play any sports?" or "What is your favorite band?" Everyday statements will also vary according to the gender, age, and maturity of the student. Using compliments and everyday statements freely opens up communication among peers, boosts self-confidence, increases the likelihood of making friends, and hopefully, enjoying success within the school environment.

Strategy 15

Learn to Use Positive Affirmations

To affirm means to declare that something is true. The statements that people make about themselves are called affirmations.

At the beginning of a school year it is common for students who appear to be unmotivated to say things like, "I'm awful at this." When learners affirm these thoughts it will probably impact their progress. A more productive affirmation is, "I'm not real comfortable with this yet, but I know with practice I will be."

Self-talk can have a huge impact on one's consciousness. It is very important to learn how to self-monitor statements about oneself so that students, as well as others, will believe that with practice and hard work anything is possible.

Using positive affirmations regularly usually becomes a life-long habit. Other people enjoy being around individuals who are positive, upbeat and happy. When individuals give off "clear, positive messages" versus "muddy, negative messages" it greatly boasts one's popularity and consequently one's desire to go to school with a more motivated attitude.

Below list 5 positive affirmations one could use when needing to learn new or difficult school information.

1. _____

_____

2. _____

_____

3. _____

_____

4. _____

_____

5. _____

_____

Strategy 16

Assertive Questions to Clarify One's Understanding

Sometimes students are reluctant to ask their teachers to explain information more simply. When students do not fully understand the basic framework of the learning objective, than with each passing day the subject matter becomes harder and harder to learn.

It can be very useful to practice certain phrases and/or questions in an assertive but polite tone. Listed below are 5 examples of useful phrases and questions to practice saying in a confident, assertive tone when a student needs further clarification or review. Ask these questions as soon as more help is needed.

1. "I am confused. Is there a time I can ask you some questions?"

2. "Could you repeat that one more time?"

3. "To make sure my notes are correct, would you look at them after class?"

4. "Are you planning a review session?"

5. "I am not sure I understand."

List below 5 more phrases that you are likely to use. Practice using an assertive, polite tone.

1. _____

_____

2. _____

_____

3. _____

_____

4. _____

_____

5. _____

_____

Strategy 17

Interviewing Peers

For those students who seem unmotivated, and who are chronic underachievers, give them an assignment to interview 6 of their peers. The teacher should select the students who are to be interviewed. (Select both genders, with four being strong academic students and two who are weak.)

Using the interview form on the next page, the interviewer is to ask the 15 questions, putting a check in the yes or no column based on answers to each question. Circle the B for boy or G for girl for each interviewee.

Discuss the results with the interviewee, especially any similarities among the academically stronger and weaker students. Finally, discuss similarities and differences between the interviewer and the interviewees.

Six Interviews

Circle B/boy or G/girl for each interview.

Check yes or no for each question.

	1		2		3		4		5		6	
	B	G	B	G	B	G	B	G	B	G	B	G
	yes	no	yes	no	yes	no	yes	no	yes	no	yes	no
1. Do you like school?												
2. Do you have a lot of friends?												
3. Are you a good friend?												
4. Do you have a good sense of humor?												
5. Do you like change?												
6. Do you feel in control of your school work?												
7. Do you have problems doing school work alone?												
8. Do you want to have good grades?												
9. Do you think doing well in school is important?												
10. Do you get your assignments done on time?												
11. Do you usually make good decisions?												
12. Are you looking forward to your future?												
13. Is a clean environment important to you?												
14. Do you do any community service to help others?												
15. Do you belong to any clubs or teams?												

Strategy 18

Setting Goals!

It is important, as students get older, to get into the habit of setting goals for themselves. There are short-term goals, which can be achieved during the day or week, and there are long-term goals, which may take a year or a decade to complete.

Below are examples of some short-term and long-term goals.

Short-Term Goals

Complete homework daily

Clean my room weekly

Watch the tone of my voice

Complete chores on time

Smile often!

Long-Term Goals

Pass all courses with a "B"

Get involved in school clubs

Be a good friend at school

Graduate from high school

Keep a part-time job

After sharing examples of goals, tell your students that it is now their turn!! Have them write 5 short-term and 5 long-term goals which are important to them. Discuss.

Short-term goals

1. _____

   _____

2. _____

   _____

3. _____

   _____

4. _____

   _____

5. _____

   _____

Long-term goals

1. _____

   _____

2. _____

   _____

3. _____

   _____

4. _____

   _____

5. _____

   _____

Quiet Time to Dream and Reflect

When a person gets into the habit of setting goals, reflecting upon personal effort, and dreaming about the future it motivates them to push themselves daily.

Using maps or a globe, talk about places one would like to visit. Revisit long-term goals that students selected. Discuss the strategy of setting aside a few minutes, three times a day, to close your eyes and picture oneself achieving the goal or visiting the place. The more hopeful and knowledgeable one becomes, the more obvious it is to most individuals that an education is vitally important.

Emphasize that anything worth having in life requires hard work and a positive attitude. (See the Bookmarker on left).

---

6 Principles For A
Positive
School Attitude

1. Remind myself I can have a good day or a bad day. It is up to me!

2. Send clear messages not muddy messages to others.

3. Tell myself that anything worth having requires hard work!

4. Celebrate things that make me special!

5. Challenge myself to learn new things

6. Exercise, eat well and get enough sleep.

Strategy 20

A Positive Attitude Bookmarker

It may be helpful to be reminded daily of the 6 basic principles of a positive school attitude. Xerox and laminate the bookmarker on the left for each of your students to use in their favorite school book.

Strategy 21

"Circle of Friends"

When teachers allow students to volunteer a portion of their free time to gather materials and organize an activity for a classmate, they actually help themselves to use time more wisely. Peers helping peers makes learning more fun, provides opportunities to review learning objectives, gives students avenues to make friends, builds self esteem, and can be helpful to teachers who need time to individualize instruction.

The appropriate pairing of students is important to maximize this activity. Place stronger students with weaker students, but be sure to monitor the compatibility of the pairings. Be sure to compliment and encourage both students for their efforts.

Section 2

Student
Organization

Strategy 22

Use Positive Nonverbal Signals

Teachers, and others, appreciate and respect students who try to learn and participate. However, adults should not assume all students are familiar with the nonverbal ways of communicating respect, interest and attention. Discuss and practice the following positive nonverbal signals students should use:

1. Make good eye contact.

2. Nod your head.

3. Use good posture and lean forward.

4. Practice punctuality.

5. Use appropriate facial expressions.

6. Avoid distracting habits or mannerisms.

7. Take notes.

8. Follow directions immediately.

9. Ask valuable questions.

10. Participate in discussions.

Strategy 23

Don't Procrastinate!

One word that describes many low achieving or unmotivated learners is PROCRASTINATION! When a person continually puts off requests, assignments, or duties, it allows others to look more deserving of recognition and respect.

Discuss this word, the need to self-monitor one's behavior, and the importance of short-term and long-term goals. Also, talk about the sense of relief and satisfaction that results from completing a task "ahead of time." The freedom and flexibility that is achieved from not needing to worry about meeting a deadline will make you the envy of all those who procrastinate!

After discussing the positive nonverbal signals on page 40, ask students to rate their good listening skills.

Are You Really Listening?

Students: Place an "X" by the skills that you need to do more often.

☐ 1. Be seated and quiet before class begins.

☐ 2. Look directly at the teacher.

☐ 3. Use good posture in my seat throughout class.

☐ 4. Nod to show I am listening.

☐ 5. Pay attention and have materials needed on desk.

☐ 6. Take notes.

☐ 7. Smile when appropriate.

☐ 8. Ask valuable questions.

☐ 9. Participate in discussions.

☐ 10. Avoid distracting habits such as pencil tapping.

When a student feels disorganized, this often adds to feeling overwhelmed and unmotivated. Adults can help children to set up an organizational system, at the beginning of each term, which will help provide structure and control. Below are examples of some useful tools.

Strategy 25

Tools for Organization

DESK

• Provide a basket under the chair for extra materials.

LOCKER

• Vertically place books in order of class day. Color code book jackets.

NOTEBOOK

• Use dividers for each subject.

• Color code dividers for each subject.

• Insert varied "class reminder checklists" for each subject. (strategy #27)

SEATING

• Systematically consider each student's best seat assignment.

• Keep distance between seats.

• Proximity to the teacher is good.

• Sit near a study buddy who is a mature role model.

• Have good natural light.

• Sit away from distractions.

Strategy 26

Personal Prescription

Self-Monitoring by the student, whether it is academic or behavioral, can often be achieved through the use of a personal prescription. The student and the teacher discuss which behaviors, if changed, could enable the student to better achieve school success. Prescriptions are checklists that the student reviews during the day and mentally asks if effort is being exerted to improve on a behavior.

Use index cards to create your own. Place the cards on a desk, inside a notebook, or possibly at home on a bathroom mirror or on a bedroom wall.

1. Am I in my seat?
2. Do I have my materials out for class?
3. Am I talking or touching anyone?
4. Am I listening to the teacher?
5. Am I taking notes?

1. Am I using good eye contact?
2. Am I smiling enough?
3. Am I speaking up?
4. Am I thinking good thoughts about myself and others?

Teach students to regularly review their "class reminder checklist" before entering each class. Students should keep this checklist in the front of their notebook sections. The following is an example of a "class reminder checklist."

Each teacher should distribute a checklist that is relevant to their subject and personal expectations.

Class Reminder Checklist

Before Class:

- *Make sure you have the necessary materials ready:*

  ☐ books   ☐ notebook

  ☐ homework assignment   ☐ paper

  ☐ pencil   ☐ special materials: dictionary, ruler, compass

When Class Begins:

- *Make sure you are seated before the bell rings.*
- *Be quiet and attentive with materials ready.*

During Class:

- *Make sure you are paying attention.*
- *Take notes for every 10 minute period.*
- *Participate and ask questions.*
- *Do not distract anyone!!*

End of Class:

- *Write down assignment.*
- *Make sure you take home books and materials.*
- *Set up an appointment to get extra assistance if needed.*
- *Prepare for your next class.*

Strategy 28

6 Week Self-Monitoring Chart

Students who are consistently lacking in self control may benefit from daily feedback from an adult. After discussing which behaviors (no more then 3) the student is to decrease or increase, the student can monitor each behavior by using the following page. The teacher also has a chart.

Twice a day (lunch time and at the end of the day) the student rates their behavior verbally to the teacher. If the teacher agrees that good effort has been displayed, a point is given on the chart. A student can earn two points a day, 10 points a week, and 60 points over a six week period.

If a student earns at least 45 points, at the end of six weeks, then a reward is given. Try to select a reward that will be very motivating. (For example: Dinner with the teacher!)

Strategy 29

Prioritize Daily Commitments!

Feeling overwhelmed with daily commitments can contribute to low achievement for students, anger, and possible depression. Although teachers need to introduce and practice the strategies used in this book, it is ultimately the student's responsibility to "put into action" the tools that need to be used on a consistent basis.

Setting and achieving goals takes daily effort. Students need to monitor time and prioritize daily commitments.

Listed below are 5 suggestions.

1. Learn to say no to activities that are not important.

2. Turn off the TV and phones and gain more than 30 hours per week.

3. Use calendars and daily plan sheets on pages 46-47.

4. Get plenty of sleep. Fatigue reduces the ability to deal with stress.

5. Eat properly and get regular exercise.

Brainstorm with the students 5 additional ideas that can make life seem less overwhelming.

Self-Monitoring Chart

for _____

						Total
Week 1	___ / ___ am pm	___ / ___ am pm	___ / ___ am pm	___ / ___ am pm	___ / ___ am pm	
Week 2	___ / ___ am pm	___ / ___ am pm	___ / ___ am pm	___ / ___ am pm	___ / ___ am pm	
Week 3	___ / ___ am pm	___ / ___ am pm	___ / ___ am pm	___ / ___ am pm	___ / ___ am pm	
Week 4	___ / ___ am pm	___ / ___ am pm	___ / ___ am pm	___ / ___ am pm	___ / ___ am pm	
Week 5	___ / ___ am pm	___ / ___ am pm	___ / ___ am pm	___ / ___ am pm	___ / ___ am pm	
Week 6	___ / ___ am pm	___ / ___ am pm	___ / ___ am pm	___ / ___ am pm	___ / ___ am pm	

Month of _____ Calendar

Fill in the dates and list assignments below.

Monday	Tuesday	Wednesday	Thursday	Friday	Sat./Sun.
❑	❑	❑	❑	❑	❑
❑	❑	❑	❑	❑	❑
❑	❑	❑	❑	❑	❑
❑	❑	❑	❑	❑	❑
❑	❑	❑	❑	❑	❑

Day of _____ Plan Sheet

Schedule your chores and assignments as part of your daily plans.

morning

7am _____

8am _____

9am _____

10am _____

11am _____

afternoon

12pm _____

1pm _____

2pm _____

3pm _____

4pm _____

evening

5pm _____

6pm _____

7pm _____

8pm _____

9pm _____

10pm _____

Strategy 30

You Are In Control!

We all make choices and are, therefore responsible for the outcomes. It is important to remember that each of us can make better choices by considering the consequences before making our decisions.

Introduce the personal remote control to your students. Go over the functions and choices on the remote control. Discuss how and why the remote control can improve our decision making.

This is your personal remote control.

Changer:

Remember you can change your mind if you know something doesn't seem right.

Pause

Stop and think before you decide.

Menu:

Evaluate all options before making your choice.

Fast Forward:

In your mind, fast forward to what the consequences of your decision might be.

Rewind:

Play back in your mind some decisions that didn't work out as a reminder not to make the same mistake.

Slow Motion:

Remember it's ok to take your time in making important decisions.

Power:

If it would not be a good decision, ZAP IT!

Play:

Enjoy the benefits of your good decision.

Mathis, T and Smith-Rex, S. (2001). Getting ahead: strategies to motivate and assist students. Minn., MN: Educational Media. Adapted from Copeland, Lori. (1998). Hunter and his amazing remote control activity guide. Chapin, SC: YoughLight, Inc.

Strategy 31

Push Your Focus Point!

Listening and concentration during class time is very tiring, even for adults. By stimulating any one of your senses: (visual, auditory, tactile, kinesthetic, olfactory, and gustatory), a person can often wake themselves up and self-monitor their ability to refocus their attention on the learning process. Think of your brain, which is stimulated by your senses, as a computer that can be programmed.

There are pressure points on your body that can be stimulated by the sense of touch. One can awaken the ability to concentrate and refocus by pushing on a pressure point. The mind has an amazing ability to make the connection that the stimulation of a pressure point (such as the one on the forearm) means to pay attention and refocus the mind into a listening/concentrating mode.

Strategy 32

Snap and Squeeze for Concentration

Allow certain students to "fiddle" in a way that does not interrupt the learning process. (i.e., wear a rubber band around the wrist and snap it quietly, squeeze a nerfball, doodle, tap a pressure point on the forearm). The student can be creative in figuring out ways to unobtrusively relieve stress and stay more focused.

Strategy 33

Headphones— An Effective Prompt

As educators, we are always pursuing new methods for enabling our students to learn. One useful strategy to consider for those students who display off-task or inappropriate behaviors is to use a self-operated, auditory prompt system.

The student clips a tape recorder on their belt and wears the headphones during certain periods of instruction. At sequenced intervals the student listens to an adult prompt. Here are two examples:

For students who have difficulty remembering the order of steps to follow, the teacher's voice gives step-by-step instructions.

For students who have difficulty staying on task, the teacher's voice gives praise and an opportunity to self-monitor or evaluate.

Strategy 34

Highlighter Pens

Students always enjoy using colorful pens to highlight their work. Color coding helps motivate students to focus, particularly kinesthetic learners who need something active to do as they learn. The different colors can mean something specific, as directed by the teacher. For example, underline in RED the important people in your notes; underline in BLUE all important dates; underline in GREEN new vocabulary to be learned; and circle in PURPLE important diagrams or mind maps to be reviewed often.

Tape record daily assignments, due dates, and other important information. Provide an area in the classroom where the student can listen to the tape at appropriate times. This is also useful for students who have missed a class period or been absent for a period of time.

Strategy 35

The Tape Recorded Center

Ask students to wear a hip-pack to carry essential daily information. This organizational tool can help all students feel more in control of school materials. (student ID's, bus pass, lunch money, pencils, etc.).

Strategy 36

The Hip-Pack Organizer

A teacher who is an effective behavior manager always has a plan to handle transitional time (e.g. walking in the halls; going to the bathroom, cafeteria, playground, or buses). This is an excellent time to utilize the assistance from your peer mediators. (See strategy #74) Sometimes unmotivated students can become very motivated if they believe that others have high expectations and confidence in them. The teacher must give clear directions, communicate specific consequences, and follow-through with the enforcement of consequences. A little effort spent stating and reinforcing expectations for transitions will help you and your students to avoid problems during these daily activities.

Strategy 37

Ounce of Prevention for Transitions

Strategy 38

Clothespin Signal

There are many visual cues that teachers can give to students to communicate which tasks they are to concentrate on. Sometimes it is important that students learn to work totally independently and to keep all noise to a bare minimum. One cue that is simple, yet effective, is for the teacher to wear a clothespin when it is time for students to quiet down, work independently, and to avoid asking any questions. This silent time is conducive to getting assignments finished and to learning the rules of the classroom.

Strategy 39

The Key is Moderation!

When children stand out negatively in their social skills they are less likely to be well liked by others. It is important to understand that displaying most behaviors in moderation works best.

Using moderate, as being in the middle, discuss this simple continuum.

Mild **Moderate** **Severe**

Discuss the following 10 terms with the children. Encourage students to see the importance of finding a comfortable balance in their use of social behaviors.

1. Appearance
The way you physically present yourself in pubic

2. Eye Contact
An ability to look into the eyes of someone with whom you are talking

3. Mannerisms
Little things people do that become habits (bite nails, twist hair, burp, tap the table)

4. Nonverbal Communication
Your way of communicating through your behavior (smile, frown, roll eyes)

5. Personal Hygiene
The way you demonstrate good health

6. Personal Space
The distance you maintain when you talk

7. Posture
The position of your body

8. Punctuality
Being prompt and on time

9. Rate of Speech
The speed at which you talk

10. Voice Tone
The feelings heard in a person's voice

When various senses are stimulated, chances increase that material will be better understood, remembered longer, and later recalled when it is needed. Knowing and using strategies to make learning information easier helps students to feel more in control of their own learning and more likely to display motivated behaviors.

Teach and practice the following strategies which can be applied to all learning situations:

Strategy 40

Strengthen "Remembering" and "Recalling" Information

1. Cluster information into chunks to learn quicker.

2. Use mnemonic devices to help remember information.(strategy #41)

3. Practice and rehearse information enough to really remember it.

4. Go through the alphabet to recall information that you have trouble recalling.

5. Draw a picture, chart, or list to consolidate information to be remembered.

6. Encourage students to use a tape recorder and/or study buddy to take good notes.

7. Practice skimming newspapers and articles for answers to questions and major themes. Refer to strategies #43 & 44 for the steps to skimming and using Multi-Pass.

(Mathis & Smith-Rex, 2001)

Anything is easier to learn when it can be related to something one already knows. Sometimes students are unmotivated to try harder at school because they don't use the "tricks of the trade." Using a variety of mnemonic devices helps students to make relationships between facts. It allows a person to retrieve facts with less frustration. Review and practice some of the ideas listed below.

Strategy 41

Memorize With Ease!

1. Cluster information to be memorized into chunks of 5 facts.

2. Make up humorous acronyms to learn a list of terms.

3. Draw a diagram, map or chart to represent the main ideas.

4. Make up a poem or song with the information.

Strategy 42

Common Pointers for Students— Cues Used by Teacher

Explain to your students that when they hear or see their teachers use the following cues, sit up and pay attention!! The information is probably important and they may be tested on it. They need to watch for the cues on the right that teachers often use so they will catch the most important facts and improve their chances of success in virtually any classroom.

Share a discussion with the students as to other cues commonly used by teachers. Staying alert, participating, and taking good notes is not an easy process. However, learning these basic skills will help anyone throughout their adult life.

Emphasis Cues:

- Changes his/her tone of voice
- Information is written on the board
- Teacher uses examples
- Teacher spells words
- Information is handed out in a study guide
- Teacher speaks more slowly so you have time to write
- Teacher stresses certain words
- Teacher uses gestures to really emphasize a point

Verbal Cues:

- "You'll probably see this again."
- "This is an important fact."
- "Pay careful attention."
- "I want to stress the following."
- "Let me repeat this."
- "To sum it up."
- "Make sure this is in your notes."

Strategy 43

Skimming for Basic Information

- Quickly move your eyes from line to line and from sentence to sentence.
- Stop when you think you've found what you are looking for.
- Read slowly the exact part of the line that tells you the answer.
- Think about the question you were finding an answer for.
- Without wasting time, write down the answer to the question.

Skimming is reading very fast for the basic facts. When you skim information by the page or paragraph, you are quickly looking at sentences for answers to your questions. When you skim you:

It is very helpful to practice this strategy often. Have students use newspapers and interesting magazines to allow practice and to motivate students to see that this will be a strategy they will use their entire life.

Strategy 44

Multi-Pass

The Multi-Pass Strategy (Deshler, 1984) encourages students to pass through a reading assignment a multitude of times, even if it isn't read word for word. This allows the student to receive a general overview of the chapter or article. Students are taught to look for information which is critical to the basic understanding of the material. It is important to pass through their assignment a multitude of times to gather major points. Have students practice this strategy by passing through the chapter doing the following:

- Read questions at the end of the chapter.

- Read all of the major headings.

- Read every picture, chart or graph.

- Look in the glossary and write down the definition of the italicized words. Keep the notes as part of your review for tests.

Strategy 45

Guided Notes

Taking notes in class is not an easy process. However, there are some strategies that can help the student stay more actively focused on the lecture. Guided notes are teacher-made handouts which "guide" students through a chapter or presentation. Standard cues and specific spaces are provided to write key concepts and facts. The theory behind guided notes is that youngsters who make responses often avoid becoming passive and uninvolved.

There are short-form guided notes and long-form guided notes. The short-form requires single words or short phrases. The long-form requires key concepts or ideas in sentences.

The following is an example of short-form guided notes.

Short-Form Guided Notes
8 ounces = 1 _____
16 ounces = 1 _____
2 cups = 1 _____
2 pints = 1 _____
4 cups = 1 _____
4 quarts = 1 _____
8 quarts = 1 _____

Strategy 46
The 10 Minute Rule

Teach the students the value of self monitoring class time and taking notes consistently throughout class. With this strategy, if guided notes are not provided, have the students take notes for every 10 minutes of class time. Students are held accountable for having key ideas and new vocabulary written down.

If the class is 50 minutes then divide notebook paper into 5 sections. Use regular notebook paper, and draw horizontal lines across the paper. (There is usually enough room for three sections on the front of the page and two sections on the back.) This simple strategy provides a useful tool for helping students to monitor their attention and to take notes throughout the entire class.

Most teachers speak at the rate of approximately 100 words per minute. Most people can think at about 400 words per minute. It takes self-discipline to not day-dream and miss the main points of a lecture. This simple strategy helps students to self-monitor their ability to pay attention throughout a class presentation.

Section 3

Motivational Strategies

Strategy 47

Motivation

Individual Characteristics That Facilitate Resiliency

1. Feeling of self-worth

2. Ability to be a friend

3. "Good at Something"

4. Sense of Humor

5. Flexible

6. Internal sense of control

7. Independent work skills

8. A connection to learning

9. Self-motivation

10. Good decision making

11. A positive view of the future

12. Aware of the environment

13. Gives of self in service to others

14. A personal faith in something greater than oneself

By definition the word motivate means to "stir to action." Lack of motivation often results from experiencing frequent failure. In this way some individuals develop learned helplessness (Seligman, 1975). Learned helplessness refers to a condition in which individuals who have experienced repeated failure tend to expect failure. To minimize or prevent failure, these students often set low expectations and are less hopeful about the future. How can concerned adults, whether they be teachers, counselors, parents, or other professionals, stir unmotivated children to want to learn in school? Educational literature emphasizes the importance of resilient behavior as it relates to school success and a healthy self-esteem. Part of mastering resilience is taking part in opportunities that allow us to come back from disappointments and experience control of one's success. Successful resiliency is a reinforcing behavior. When given opportunities to prove you can succeed under adverse conditions, your self-esteem grows and you internalize the ability to feel in control throughout life. Strategies of instruction which focus on enhancing the ability of individuals to become more self-determined are very helpful. Teachers need to implement approaches which decrease learned helplessness and increase one's internal sense of control and determination.

In the next column is a list of 14 characteristics of behaviors that facilitate resiliency. Make an overlay of this page and discuss these characteristics with fellow faculty, parents and students.

Assume the role of comedian David Letterman. His time-honored routine on his late evening show where he reads off the top reasons for something (in this case school) might be familiar to many of your students. Have some fun exploring the humorous possibilities that exist regarding school attendance and adult life.

Begin by creating an overlay that will allow you to display each reason as you work your way from number 10 to number 1 with your students and explore the humor and the truth behind each statement. You may even have some comic genius in the class who may want to add to the list.

Sometimes, we get so serious about school and schooling that children don't believe that humor and laughter can exist as a part of the discussion. Yes, it is serious business, but all of us benefit from laughing on occasion at ourselves, and, yes, even our beliefs.

Strategy 48
The Letterman Top Ten (reasons to go to school)

Top 10 Reasons to Go to School

10. If you've never been caught passing notes, there's a job for you at the FBI.

9. If you survive a school sponsored fieldtrip, you should be favored to win on "Survivor."

8. If you can leave the principal's office without crying, you will laugh at Simon when he says you're lousy!

7. By learning to wake up quickly and dress in less than a minute to get to school, you'll be fully qualified as a fire fighter.

6. By learning to ride your school's bus system, you'll be ready for the New York City subway.

5. By carrying heavy backpacks through school hallways, you'll be conditioned to move your own furniture throughout your lifetime.

4. By mastering the art of pretending to be interested, you will be prepared for years of dating conversations.

3. By learning to accept your teacher's criticism, you can laugh when Donald Trump says, "You're Fired."

2. By waiting for bathroom breaks, you will be able to train your bladder to endure long business meetings.

1. By learning to consume cafeteria food, you will be able to win the food competition in "Fear Factor."

Strategy 49

Late Bloomers are Sometimes the Most "Brilliant" Flowers

Sometimes students believe what our media often implies, that success requires not only perfection, but early and consistent perfection. Our culture often emphasizes winning and "success" without acknowledging that the process that leads to most accomplishments is anything but a straight line. People not only overcome failures, they learn and profit from them!

In this strategy, introduce students to famous people of achievement who experienced failure and obstacles in their lives. It is especially important to discuss what is most important, "Where you start, or where you end up?"

Share the accompanying list of famous people. Ask the students to match the individual with the obstacle that they struggled with during their younger years. Discuss the list and see if they can describe persons they know or have heard of who overcame difficulty.

Answer Key:
G	I
H	O
M	C
B	E
L	J
N	D
A	F
K	

Two books to consider by Tom Carr are:
Every Child Has A Gift and *Monday Morning Messages*. Available through YouthLight, Inc.

Late Bloomers

☐ Abraham Lincoln   ☐ Babe Ruth

☐ Beethoven   ☐ Bruce Jenner

☐ Albert Einstein   ☐ Winston Churchill

☐ Cher   ☐ Henry Winkler

☐ Tom Cruise   ☐ Sylvester Stallone

☐ Nelson Rockefeller   ☐ Henry Ford

☐ Robin Williams   ☐ Suzanne Somers

☐ Walt Disney

a. an actor who had ADHD (Mork)

b. a singer with a learning disability

c. once a prime minister with a learning disability

d. failed in business before success

e. "The Fonz" with a learning disability

f. female star from the 1970's with a learning disability

g. lost elections but then became a president

h. famous composer who had a learning disability

i. set records-home runs/&strikeouts

j. "Rocky" who had a learning ability

k. bankrupt then built Disneyland

l. "Top Gun" but had a learning disability

m. didn't speak until 7 but a genius

n. famous NYC family with a learning disability

o. won a gold medal but has a learning disability

Strategy 50

Peer Exploration of Interest Areas

Most students have out-of-school interests or "passion areas." All too often, it is difficult for teachers to learn about these and to utilize them as themes or subjects to help motivate their students.

Many times students will confide in peers more readily than adults when discussing their interests. By assigning students to conduct interviews of their classmates, the teacher will generate interest inventories for all students while providing students with the opportunity to practice interview and recording skills.

Teachers should carefully pair students so that an additional benefit of this strategy will be an opportunity for students who do not know each other well, or who might not otherwise interact, to share interests and get to know each other on a more personal level.

Copy the attached interview inventory for your students to use as they create the inventories for your classroom. Use the inventories to help you shape and choose motivating assignments, topics and content throughout the school year. Also, consider using the inventory information to implement the strategy #51 described, "Creating Resident Experts."

Student Interest Inventory

Name _____   Birthday_____

Interviewer _____

1. What is your favorite way to spend time after school?

_____

_____

_____

2. What is your idea of a perfect vacation?

_____

_____

_____

3. What do you collect?

_____

_____

_____

4. What is your most important possession? Why?

_____

_____

_____

5. If you could write a book about anything what would it be?

_____

_____

_____

6. Is there a subject or area of interest you know something about that you'd like to know more about? If yes, what is that subject? (For example: baseball, soccer, dinosaurs, fishing, fashion, stamps, rap music, pets, etc.)

_____

_____

_____

Strategy 51

Creating "Resident Experts"

Through the use of the previous strategy, "Peer Exploration of Interest Areas," and through informal discussions, parent conferences, and written assignments it is often possible to discover that students possess an in-depth knowledge about certain topics and/or a keen interest in learning more about topics of high interest to them. For all students, but especially for underachievers, it is highly motivating to be encouraged by a teacher to study further about their topics of special interest and to be designated as the school's "Resident Expert." This not only boosts motivation and self-confidence, it provides enhanced research and study skills.

As part of the acknowledgement of your resident experts, create a database of topics and experts to distribute to every teacher in the school. These students can become valuable resources to teachers and can provide "Resident Expert" presentations for their own, and other, classes. Provide assistance to your experts as they study their topics of interest and, when appropriate, prepare presentations. Most will need some structure as they plan for their research and enhance their expertise.

Strategy 52

"A Picture Is Worth A Thousand Words"

The game of charades can be an exciting way for students to expand vocabulary, explore analogies, foster creativity and learn teamwork. By choosing appropriate song titles, television programs, and movie titles; by carefully designing teams; and, by matching students to difficulty levels, you can create a learning experience that will provide not only enjoyment, but successes for all students.

Design your teams so that you have an equitable balance of strong students and weaker students. Avoid creating teams made up of close friends and allies. Mix students who would not voluntarily spend time together and check to see that the diversity present in your classroom (eg. socio-economic, ethnicity, gender, etc.) is fairly represented across teams.

Use the titles listed to create "coded" and folded slips to be "drawn" by the teacher for contestants to act out. The key here is the difficulty codes of #1, #2, or #3 that will be on the outside of the slip that enables the teacher to pick slips with appropriate difficulty levels for students. Match the difficult levels well and you help increase the probability that every student, and team, will compete effectively during this strategy.

Assign a #1, #2, or #3 for difficulty codes for each song, tv show, or movie.

Select the # based on the approximate ability level of each student.

Songs

Where's the Love

Stronger

Yeah!

Milkshake

I Can Only Imagine

Come Clean

Jenny From the Block

Concrete Angel

Rock Your Body

Landslide

TV

American Idol

Knock First

Survivor

Seventh Heaven

Bachelor

Will & Grace

Friends

Switched

Recess

Proud Family

Movies

The Prince and Me

Bring It On

Cheaper by the Dozen

Charlie's Angels

Freaky Friday

Mona Lisa Smile

Fast and Furious

Blue Crush

DareDevil

Finding Nemo

Strategy 53

Seeing Is Believing

All research done in the past fifty years regarding the impact and importance of nonverbal communication is consistent. It is powerful and it matters to all of us. Many times students aren't aware of the non-verbal messages they are sending- sometimes to their extreme disadvantage.

It can be both fun and informative for the teacher to explore with students the messages that are sent through voice intonation, facial expressions, body posture, clothing choices, etc. Assigned skills can contrast how a situation utilizing exactly the same verbal messages (verbatim), but differing nonverbally, can convey totally different messages to the audience. For example, a verbal compliment, given with supporting voice intonation, facial expression and body posture versus the same spoken statement with flat intonation, negative or blank facial expression, and contradictory body posture (e.g. arms folded) will quickly show students the human inclination to always choose to believe the nonverbal message over the verbal message when they are contradictory.

Discuss the significance of this human preference and why it exists. Discuss the implications of sayings such as, "two-faced," "walk the talk," "practice what you preach" and the desire by many to see a face or even to look into the eyes of someone who is saying something that is deemed to be important or critical.

All of us, teachers, students, parents and others place a great deal of significance upon "how" things are said. We can all profit from paying more attention to how our nonverbal messages are sent, and received.

Strategy 54

The Bandwagon— Propaganda Technique— Going Along for the Ride

Teaching our students about how advertisers, politicians, and others utilize the Bandwagon approach in attempts to influence us to purchase a certain product, elect a specific individual, or endorse a lifestyle choice can have multiple benefits by helping students be more analytic in responding to external messages. It can also provide an opportunity for discussing the merits and liabilities of choosing to "go along." Sometimes choosing to fit in is a positive choice, but under certain circumstances, it can be a poor decision.

Give examples of advertisements, commercials and political ads that use the Bandwagon approach. Examples such as: "the number one selling product; the leading candidate; the most popular…; everyone is doing or wearing it;" will provide opportunities to discuss if these techniques work, and why. You will also be able to discuss how this effects your students' behavior and choices. Are they aware of this influence upon them and their peers? What can they do to be sure that they will make choices for valid reasons?

Strategy 55

"Snap Shotting" Opinions and Values— Nonverbal Classroom Polls

All of us appreciate having our opinions "count." At its basic level, that is what democracy is built upon—the premise that every opinion matters.

All too often, passive and underachieving students don't believe their opinions matter, or that they can compete with students who are more assertive or, perhaps, more verbally gifted. An effective way for the teacher to give all students a way to respond to carefully crafted value statements is to structure nonverbal classroom polls.

After presenting a value-laden statement such as, "girls are better at teamwork than boys," or "intelligent life exists on other planets in our universe," students are asked to nonverbally respond by choosing one of the following nonverbal displays and continuing that display for 20 seconds (so that everyone can look around the classroom and take a nonverbal "snapshot" of how the entire group feels about the topic):

What this strategy does is to allow everyone to display his or her opinion quickly and in a non-intimidating way. It also opens up wonderful opportunities for follow-up discussion by the teacher and the class. In fact, important insights can be drawn from the teacher and/or students explicating the meaning and rationale behind their choice of thumb position. (Yes, the teacher should display his/her nonverbal reaction to the statement, but only after the 20 second time period).

When a discussion is full and enlightening on a topic it is often useful to reiterate the statement and to once again take the nonverbal classroom poll. When changes occur (as they often do) discuss why people changed their response and the importance of being able to change one's position. Also explore why the prerequisites to changing a viewpoint are often information and discussion and why this is important to us as individuals and as a nation.

Agree – thumb up

Disagree – thumb down

Strongly agree – thumb up and shaking

Strongly disagree – thumb down and shaking

Learning How to Engage in Inquiry-Riddles

Most of us love a mystery—especially if we know that the answer is knowable and that we can find it! Learning how to ask good questions is often more important then providing answers. Students can learn how to enjoyably engage in group inquiry through the solving of mystery riddles, utilizing "yes" and "no" responses from the teacher to their questions.

By initially asking the class as a group to solve the riddles, the less assertive students can observe and then learn how the problems are being solved by the more assertive and sophisticated students. After the class has solved a number of riddles, you may want to call on students to ask questions, or create competitive questioning teams to ensure fuller participation.

Once students learn how to "efficiently" ask questions and move towards solving your riddles, they will look forward to these "mental exercises." Consider doing this for the first ten minutes of class or to introduce a unit. It is an enjoyable way to show how important inquiry is in solving problems.

Below are two examples of riddles for upper elementary through high school:

A man's body is found in the desert.
He died within the last twenty-four hours.
There are no visible wounds on the body.
There are no footprints near the body and
he did not die from natural causes.
How did he die?

(Answer: Parachutist whose chute failed)

Anthony and Kylie are found lying dead.
They are found dead in the middle
of a room surrounded by broken glass.
The cause of death is suffocation.
How did they die?

(Answer: They are two gold fish.
A cat knocked the fish bowl off of
the table and it broke on the floor.)

Sample books that include riddles for children and adolescents:

"201 Amazing Mind Bogglers"
YouthLight Publishing Co. Inc., Chapin, S.C.

"The little giant book of riddles", 1996
"The little book of mini mysteries", 1997
"The little giant book of whodunits", 1998
Sterling Publishing Co. Inc., New York is also a publisher for riddle books.

Strategy 57

Seeing Ourselves

To see ourselves as others see us provides insight for change and improvement. Unfortunately, this rarely happens for most of us outside of specialized professions such as areas of the performing arts.

How we "perform" in our classrooms has significant impact upon our success or failure to achieve our goals with our students. A non-threatening way to engage in serious self-evaluation is to set up a video camera in the back of your room and let it run unnoticed for two or three hours. If you find it difficult to accomplish this in a low-key way with your students, leave the camera set up for a number of days before you tape "for real." The students will tire of the novelty of the camera in a few days.

When you review the video of you in the classroom you will discover many things about your own teaching style and about the interaction between yourself and your students. Be especially sensitive to the verbal and nonverbal responses you are giving and whether or not you are unintentionally ignoring some students. Sometimes unmotivated students just need a little more reinforcement!

Strategy 58

Enhancing Motivation Through Nontraditional Recognition

A significant number of students are not motivated by the traditional incentives and awards found in our schools. Academic grades, teachers' recognition and even peer approval fall short for some students. The challenge lies not only in the array of incentives and rewards customarily utilized, but also in the limited number of behaviors, accomplishments and personal characteristics chosen for recognition.

While academic achievement, content mastery, and competence must continue to be highly valued and rewarded by schools and teachers, other accomplishments and characteristics can also be acknowledged as important and necessary.

Consider approaching local businesses and civic organizations with a request for rewards for outstanding student categories in your classroom. They would receive publicity for their support and should be invited to attend the class period in which the recognition would be awarded and the rewards presented. The rewards could be meals (restaurants), gift certificates, products (retail or wholesale) services (service providers), etc.

In addition to tradional academic recognitions, "top ten" awards can be awarded to students who demonstrated a special or unique talent such as: effort, empathy, improvement, helpfulness, positive attitude, inquisitiveness, peer buddy, courage, leadership or friendliness. The teacher can determine the criteria for each and may want to also solicit nominations from peers and teachers. The "pomp and circumstance" around "award ceremonies" is up to the teacher. It is a wonderful opportunity for the teacher, and others (testimonials) to speak about why a student is receiving an award. Not every award need be granted each time and, while it is ideal if every student receives at least one award over time, the rationale for a recognition must be transparent to students or the credibility of the effort will be in question.

Strategy 59

What's Up? Using Contemporary News To Learn Functional Skills

It's no secret that most American children watch a great deal of television. Many critics feel our students watch too much television and that it is a question of quality as well as quantity. It's also notable that few students, and adults, find the time to keep up with and understand contemporary issues through television and/or newsprint.

An assignment for students that enables each to identify and report on a news story of interest to them that they have seen on television or read about in the newspaper is a way to direct attention to contemporary issues and to teach important functional skills. By setting aside 15 minutes each day for reports and discussion, every student should be able to identify a topic or event of interest and to orally summarize the specifics and the importance of their choice.

Students will practice the skills of summarization, analysis, and public speaking. In addition, vocabulary, listening skills, questioning skills and the level of contemporary knowledge about a range of issues will benefit from the "reporting" and discussions.

Strategy 60

Up Close and Personal— Make Faculty/Student Connections

If we want students to care about what we think of them and their behavior in our classroom, our odds improve if they believe we care about them as individuals. The operative word here is "believe." How do we "convince" students that we view them as individuals and have a genuine concern for their welfare? The answers depend upon the personal characteristics of the student and the teacher. People respond differently to overtures from others, but there are some strategies that capitalize on universal human tendencies.

We all know the importance of knowing and using a person's name, but that is only the beginning. Learn as much as you can about the students' personal circumstances: parents(s) name(s), siblings(s) names, home address, personal interests, unique positive and negative personal experiences. This can be done through private one-on-one conversations, parent interviews, a journal, written assignments, and interest inventories (strategy #3).

Once you have this information, use it! Let the student know, on a regular basis that you are aware of him/her, their history, their personal circumstances, their challenges in life, and their "uniqueness." Do this with comments and personal notes. Contact (phone, visit, write) parent(s) or guardians throughout the school year to let them know that you continue to be interested in their young person. The student will know about these contacts and, whether they acknowledge it directly or not, it will make an important difference in how they perceive you and your role as teacher.

Finally, keep in mind that we all care more about what the people who are a part of our life think about us, as opposed to strangers. You can't become a family member or "buddy" to your students, but you can become much, much more than a stranger. As an informed, personally engaged professional you dramatically increase your ability to persuade and motivate your underachieving students.

Strategy 61

Combating Isolation: Inclusion of Underachievers

"Loneliness and the feeling of being unwanted is the most terrible poverty."

—Mother Teresa

Underachievers and poorly motivated students are often students with one or more of the following: poor socialization skills, poor self-concepts, and low self-worth. Teachers, counselors and others often find the reason for these problems to be both complex and persistent. What can a teacher do to help a student overcome or lessen the negative effects of such deficiencies?

The answer is inclusion. The teacher has power in his or her classroom to assign status and credibility to individuals through a variety of formal and informal actions. Conversely, the teacher can cause a student to lose status and credibility (often unintentionally) by verbal and nonverbal behaviors. By ignoring a student or reacting negatively verbally or nonverbally to a student, the teacher can assign a negative status to a student that can strengthen and perpetuate the isolation of that student.

Use this important teacher power to assign positive status by assigning a special responsibility to isolated students in the presence of their peers. Look for opportunities for leadership role assignments for isolated students. Make a consistent and persistent effort to display positive verbal and nonverbal responses to the identified student. Take time to have one-on-one discussions and send positive notes home. Encourage social and team interactions with other students through cooperative learning and experiential learning activities (see strategies #62 and #63).

It is virtually impossible to be motivated to learn in an environment where one feels unaccepted, ignored, or demeaned. In the classroom, no other individual has the power of the classroom teacher to change this devastating dynamic. Use this power wisely and you can dramatically and positively effect young lives.

In the adult world, much of our learning and working takes place as members of groups or teams. There is ample evidence that many students can be more successful in school through forms of cooperative learning.

Instead of always expecting students to study, learn, and perform as individuals, organize them into teams of two or more. Experiment with different degrees of self-selection and teacher-selection for team formation, but attempt to ensure acceptable levels of parity if team outcomes are to be presented and/or compared.

Cooperative learning not only enables many students a more effective way to master content, it also teaches

Strategy 62
Cooperative Learning— Teaming for Success!

teaming and socialization skills that are extremely valuable. This approach can also sometimes pair poorly motivated students with more highly motivated students who can, through subtle modeling, help bring about positive changes in the weaker student.

> "You can discover more about a person in an hour of play than in a year of conversation."
>
> —Plato

While the classroom environment can be significantly adapted to enhance motivation and learning, it does have its limitations. Sometimes moving outside of the classroom for learning activities is, in itself, a motivator—for students and teachers alike. The options are many here, and they range from going outside onto the school grounds to an extended field trip.

Many schools have and are working with organizations to construct ropes courses (known by many names such as challenge courses, adventure courses, etc.) on school property to facilitate experiential education experiences. Often, such courses already exist in communities at non-profits, churches, camps, YMCA's and educational institutions. Most accept and accommodate outside groups, usually for a very modest fee.

It is important to always remember that the physical space that we describe as a classroom has, as do all physical spaces, a set of limitations. We can, however,

Strategy 63
Experiental Learning Activities

provide many hands-on, experiental experiences for students within that space and an even greater variety of experiences outside of that space.

Most of us do not think creatively enough about how to provide more hands-on experiences for our students. Not only is this approach a way to enliven and motivate underachieving students, it provides increased learning and comprehension for all students. An outstanding resource for learning more about this approach is through "Project Adventure," an interdisciplinary program that involves experience-based learning in academics that includes a variety of alternative programs for both indoor and outdoor settings.

Contact: Project Adventure, Inc., P.O. Box 100, Hamilton, MA. 01936, (508) 468-7981

Strategy 64

Sneak Previews of Coming Attractions

All learners benefit from being told, in advance, what is being planned for them and what will be expected of them. This may be especially true for students who are poorly motivated and/or have difficulty focusing on academic routine and assignments.

Advanced organizers can be written or orally provided. The ideal is usually a combination of the two. These should be provided regularly at the beginning of class periods and academic units. They need not be lengthy, but they should be regularly reinforced and updated-especially when there are modifications.

The basic ingredients of advance organizers include – what we will be doing (content); how long will it take (schedule); why we are doing this (rationale); what will be expected of you (learner expectations/outcomes); and how you will be evaluated (measurements). Not surprisingly, most of us want to know "whas up?" in our lives. This is especially true when others are in control. Be sure that your students always know where you and they are headed in your classroom. This will significantly increase the odds of your mutual success!!

Strategy 65

Personalization—
A Powerful Tool

Most accomplished motivational speakers include personal anecdotes and stories in their presentation repertoires. They know that all of us like stories and we especially like stories that give us an insight into the personal life of the speaker or presenter.

In many respects, teachers are motivational speakers. Of course, it is one thing to have a "well practiced" thirty minute presentation and quite another to be in front of a classroom for extended periods of time every day. Nonetheless, we all need to look for those teachable moments, even those inspirational opportunities, that present themselves to us on a regular basis with our students.

Teachers who tell their students about themselves will find, sometimes to their astonishment, that students are truly interested. This can be a powerful tool when the revelations are related to a challenge, or problem, that the students are experiencing themselves. "Once, when I was your age," can be a captivating introduction, especially if you describe a weakness, insecurity, or failure that you experienced.

Students often never imagine their teacher as being fallible or challenged as an adult, or as a child. The realization that even "you" wrestle with the same human struggles that confront them can build a stronger relationship and motivate students to not only try harder, but to be more likely to share with you, and others, their concerns about succeeding in life.

Try It! If a picture is worth a thousand words, a personalized story, well told, with a moral or lesson can be worth a thousand lectures or directives.

Strategy 66

The Music of Learning

The power of music is undeniable. It not only "soothes the "savage beast" it calms us, excites us, inspires us, disturbs us, and, sometimes, even enables us. We have a friend who always exercises to the music from the movie, "Rocky." She swears it motivates her even on her worst days to make it through her routine.

Most of our students listen to music. It has important meaning to many of them. Often, that meaning is further enhanced by lyrics. It may or may not be easy for teachers to relate to, or even understand, some of the popular music and lyrics that students enjoy; but (here in) lies a potentially powerful ally in our efforts to motivate students.

For example, some students who will moan and groan about the prospect of reading and explaining written poetry will enthusiastically play, read and explain the meaning of the lyrics in their favorite song. And, believe it or not, some of these are as thought provoking and controversial as anything in a college American Literature course!

Of course, the teacher must use some discretion in the selections allowed, but once the ground rules are set and explained, you will be surprised at the variety and quality of many of the songs nominated by your students. You may want to select some of your favorites for inclusion also.

The options here are many. You may want to simply set aside some time each day or each week for "approved" songs to be played and the lyrics (preferably typed and handed out) discussed by the presenter and the class.

You may want to turn this unit into a "music festival" of sorts where the class votes on which songs were the most thought provoking, humorous, romantic, inspirational, etc.

Finally, for older students, and where resources allow, the music selected can become a multi-media presentation, where the students individually, or in pairs, use slides or video to supplement the lyrics and/or music and 'produce" presentations for the class and/or school.

Remember, most of our students are listening to, and thinking about, contemporary music. Whether their tastes are country-western or rap, these are songs to which they and their friends attach meaning. When we find legitimate ways to utilize that meaning within our classrooms as part of our instructional goals, we introduce a powerful medium and a powerful motivational force.

Section 4

Teachers' Strategies

Discipline/Engagement

Strategy 67

Selecting the Most Appropriate Student/ Teacher "Fit"

Underachievers typically do their worst in classes in which there is a poor "connection" between the teacher and the student. Because of varied teaching styles, discipline methods, and classroom environments, it is very important for counselors and principals to NOT randomly place the more "at risk" student in just any classroom. By closely examining each teacher's personal style and the student's specific needs, many motivational problems can be avoided.

Strategy 68

"E" is for Effort

Most of us recognize the merit of a genuinely strong effort to reach a goal or accomplish a mission—even when one falls short of reaching the objective. We also know that, due to circumstances and/or inherent ability, some goals are achieved with little or no real effort.

Most formal grading systems are oriented towards certifying and measuring the achievement of curricular goals and specific skills (e.g. learning standards). While these symbols (e.g. A,B,C,D,F) can be motivating for students who are experiencing degrees of success, they can sometimes disillusion or frustrate those students who may be putting forth significant effort, but experiencing little mastery.

One strategy for giving students fair and objective feedback on mastery, while also recognizing the degree of effort put forth is to compliment the mastery grade with the letter "E" where you feel it is justified.

This compliment can be attached to any letter grade, for example from A to F. You are being truthful with the student about the mastery achieved and you are recognizing the outstanding effort whether or not it is linked to a high level of mastery of a particular skill. For some students, this can be a powerful motivator. The teacher knows this "A" was the result of a great deal of work on my part, or, I still don't get it but at least the teacher knows I really am trying hard and it is not indifference or laziness that's the problem.

All of us are motivated by a special pat on the back when we experience success as a result of extra effort and, equally, by applause when we slip or fall short while striving towards a goal. Adding an "E" to your grading system will give you another tool to motivate your students and to symbolically reinforce the virtue of "an E for Effort."

Strategy 69

Predictable-Positive Discipline

The need is critical for a discipline program that works with today's students. Disorder in the classroom threatens American education. Teachers and parents need to shift their thinking from control to cooperation and from intimidation to encouragement. It is our responsibility, as caring adults, to do our best to ensure that all children feel good about themselves. The degree of success that is achieved in the school is directly proportional to the quality of the relationships that are developed.

Keep in mind the following major points:

1. Classroom rules should always be carefully explained to students and parents. Clearly post the rules and use the rules consistently, quickly, and fairly.

2. If rules are clearly communicated then there should be no need for adults to overreact to inappropriate behavior.

3. Adults should use a calm approach by avoiding too much emotion or discussion.

4. Adults want to make a positive "connection" with each student. It is most important, even when angry or frustrated, to avoid sarcasm and ridicule.

5. Consider using a 4 Step Discipline Model in order to be prepared for all levels of behavior.

   1. Empathic Listening

   2. Assertive Discipline Training

   3. Use of Cueing and basic sign language to lower noise

   4. Crisis Intervention Training

   See the next 4 strategies.

Strategy 70

Empathic Listening

When a person uses empathic listening you must **Listen** for the **Feeling** which is displayed. Using that feeling word, "mirror back" a statement that lets the child know that you hear him/her and are not being judgmental.

For example:

The child says,

"I hate school."

The teacher/parent responds by:

1. Using the word hate/dislike.
2. Mirror back a question.

"You dislike school?"

The child will probably give you more information as to why he/she feels the way he does. This becomes the foundation for building a "connection." Use empathic listening as often as possible. Although at times it may seem tedious, it is a useful tool for opening lines of communication with others.

"What" and "how" questions work better than "why" questions with children.

Consider Lee Canter's Assertive Discipline Approach (Canter, 1982), Thomas Phelan's Approach, Fred Jones's Approach, or Harry Wong's. All systems are based on a systematic approach utilizing basic behavior modification principles. The programs focus generally on two things: how to stop negative behaviors and how to start positive behaviors. The success of the programs hinge upon reducing the amount of talk and emotion expended by the adult in charge. Immediate and consistent consequences or rewards are provided. This in turn shapes the desired behaviors.

If your school doesn't have an assertive program in place in each classroom, try implementing one of these. Assertive discipline is a very important component to the 4 step model.

Using the following two pages, teach your students a few basic signs, which is a useful tool in the classroom. Signs can be used by teachers to nonverbally communicate messages to students.

Begin by deciding if you want to teach the alphabet. It is useful because the students realize why signs are what they are. Secondly, teach the students the 12 signs which follow. This can be just the beginning!!

Alphabet

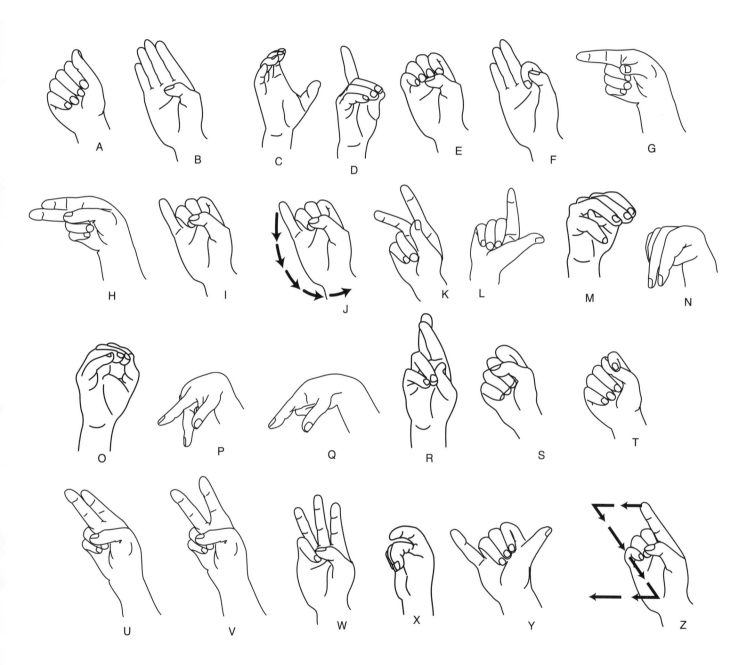

Signs

Sign Language is a useful tool in the classroom. Signs can be used
by teachers to nonverbally communicate messages to students.

Come: With your index fingers out, roll out hands towards your body.

Yes: Move your fist up and down in front of you.

Quiet: Begin with your finger on your lips. Move hand down and away from the mouth.

Good: Place the tips of your fingers of your right hand on your chin and move your hand out to meet your left palm.

No: Bring your index and middle finger together in one motion to your thumb.

Stop: Chop your right hand into the palm of your left.

Sit Down: Both open hands are held palms down and fingers pointing forward. Move hands down a short distance.

Help: Close the left hand in fist. Lift the left hand with an open right hand.

Work: Both hands are made into fists. The right hand strikes the top of the left hand several times.

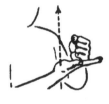

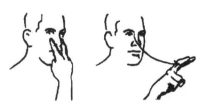

Try: Put your thumbs between your index and middle fingers. In a circular motion, touch your chest and push out.

Look: Point to your eyes, then twist your hand and point in the desired direction.

Line Up: Face palms of hands together. Move hands apart, right hand toward the chest and left outward.

from Smith-Rex, Susan and Frank, "Tip"

Strategy 73

Nonviolent Crisis Intervention

Teachers are best able to provide a secure environment when they also feel secure. By inservicing staff with Nonviolent Crisis Intervention it helps adults develop the basic therapeutic physical intervention skills necessary to manage students with more severe behavioral needs. This program presents techniques as well as a philosophy of care and welfare.

Nonviolent Physical Crisis Intervention is used only as a last resort, however when adults have gone through the training it raises their self confidence, their assertiveness skills, and hopefully a desire to "connect" with specific students with more serious needs.

For more information contact:
National Crisis Prevention Institute, Inc.
3315 – K North 124th St.
Brookfield, WI. 53005
1-800-558-8976

Strategy 74

Using Secret Ballots To Select Peer Mediators

At the end of a lesson on self-esteem and leadership, have the students write on their ballot the name of one boy and one girl who demonstrates fairness and good leadership skills on a regular basis.

Count the votes! The two boys and the two girls with the most votes will be considered the class peer mediators. (There will be 4 peer mediators per class.)

Peer mediation tends to work better when the students, rather than the teacher, select who they would accept as a mediator to address a problem.

The 4 peer mediators from each class will participate in a fifty-minute lesson to prepare them for becoming a class peer mediator. An outline of this lesson is on page 85. For training purposes it is best to not mix grade levels.

Peer Mediator Training Guide

1. Distribute Peer Mediator nametags and congratulate each student on being selected by their peers for this honor.

2. Provide each student with the handout "A Conflict Manager" listed below.

3. Do some role-playing of situations that might occur in school that the peer mediators could assist with in solving the conflict. Emphasize the following points:

   • Treat each other with respect. You are Not the boss!

   • Your role is to encourage classmates to peacefully talk out disagreements.

   • Never try to stop a physical fight. Go get your teacher or other adult.

   • If classmates can resolve a problem, then the peer mediator does not need to go to the teacher of the students involved.

   • Show understanding through nonverbal behaviors such as: eye contact, straight posture, nod, and calm expressions.

The basic questions and statements to use in the role-playing situations include:

1. "It looks like you might be having a disagreement."

2. "Tell each other quietly why you are upset." (Each student takes a turn while the peer mediator listens with an open mind and without interruption.)

3. Ask the big question: "Can you both work this out?" (If both students agree, then the issue is over and is not to be discussed further. If either student says "No", the peer mediator describes the issue to the teacher.

4. Distribute parental permission letters.

5. Ask the students to wear their peer mediator badges each day and treat their election as an honor and responsibility.

6. Tell the students that the group will convene every month for thirty minutes to be rewarded for their efforts. The school counselor should be receptive to the group on a daily basis to offer advice when needed.

A Conflict Manager:	
IS...	IS NOT...
Fair	A Judge
Helpful	A Police Officer
Respectful	A Gossip
Trustful	A Boss

Strategy 75

Helping Yourself to Help Students Contribute

When students feel a sense of contribution to their home, class, school or community they are much more likely to fulfill obligations and set positive goals.

Everyone wants to feel needed. Everyone wants to feel important. Adults who create an environment that stimulates involvement will also instill a personal satisfaction in contributing. Use the contribution wheel below to think about and identify ways that you can improve upon your ability to assist students to increase their opportunities to contribute to your classroom and their classmates. Identify the skills that you need to concentrate on to become more effective.

Examine the Contribution Wheel below. List 5 skills that you need to concentrate on to become more actively involved in helping others.

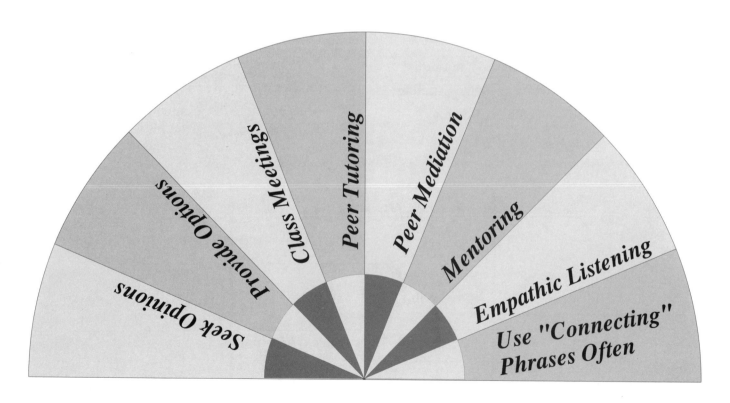

Strategy 76

Girl Talk! or Boy Talk!

A sample guide follows:

Week 1
Welcome to Girl Talk
Pre-survey
Confidentiality
Front-burner/Back-burner
(Use strategies #3 & #7)
A helpful video to show is:
"Don't Laugh At Me"
www.dontlaugh.org/curricula (free)

Week 2
Types of intelligences
You are in control
Anger management
(Use strategies #4 & #30)

Week 3
Short-term/Long-term goals
Self-monitoring behavior
(Use strategies #18 & #22-30)

Week 4
What is a true friend?
Giving compliments,
(Use strategies #12 & #14-17)

Week 5
Social skills
Forming good relationships
Nonverbal communication
(Use strategies #9-15)

Week 6
Bullying
Standing up for myself
(Use strategies #12, #13 & #74)

Week 7
Peer mediation
School leadership
Support systems
(Use strategy #74)

Week 8
Saying No to Smoking
Ways to say No
(See ordering information which follows)

Week 9
Saying No to Sex – part 1

Week 10
Saying No to Sex – part 2
(See ordering information which follows)

Week 11
Coping strategies for drug
and alcohol related issues
(See ordering information which follows)

Week 12
Closure
Post-survey
Celebration!
(Use the survey from strategy #3)

This 12 week program is an after-school club for a grade level (5th through 8th). The club leader should select a grade level and a gender to focus on. This program is for students who would like to learn ways to become better decision makers and communicators, while also feeling good about themselves.

Each week an important topic will be discussed and then practical strategies will be learned and practiced to help students apply their knowledge to their own lives.

Students will have opportunities to participate in activities that are aimed at increasing self-esteem, learning positive assertiveness skills, exploring strong social skills, discussing strong leadership skills, anger management, and why it is important to say no to sex and smoking.

Useful books to guide club leaders are published by Educational Media (763-781-0088):

1. *Getting With It – Social Skills*
2. *Getting Equipped to Stop Bullying*
3. *Getting Your Second Wind: Living a Smoke-Free Life*
4. *Saying No to Sex*
5. *Getting Ahead: Strategies to Motivate and Assist Students with Classroom Learning*

A few of the helpful books from Youth Light, Inc. (800-209-9774):

1. *The Very Angry Day That Amy Didn't Have*
2. *Josh's Smiley Faces*
3. *We Can Work It Out*

Strategy 77

Do Your Students Believe In Themselves?

We get out of life pretty much what we put into life! As Dr. Seuss said,

"You have brains in your head.
You have feet in your shoes.
You can steer yourself in any
direction that you choose."

Many students have a hard time believing in themselves and believing that they can make meaningful decisions about their lives Consider renting and showing a movie once each month that emphasizes personal courage, perseverance and self-determination. Whether it is an animated film like "Finding Nemo" or a serious look at real life obstacles like "Radio," students will be willing to discuss the film and its implications for themselves and others. Remember, with your assistance, powerful movies can teach life long lessons about personal empowerment.

Strategy 78

Remember, We Learn More From A Model Than From A Critic

15 Student Thoughts for Teachers:

1. Don't do things for me that I can do for myself.

2. Don't spoil me. I know quite well that I should not have all I ask for.

3. Don't be afraid to be firm, but fair, with me. It lets me know where I stand.

4. Don't correct me harshly in front of other people. I'll take much more notice if you talk quietly with me in private.

5. Don't demand explanations for my wrong behavior. I really don't know why I did it.

6. Don't nag. If you do, I shall have to protect myself by appearing deaf.

7. Don't try to preach to me. You'd be surprised how well I know right from wrong.

8. Don't use force with me. It teaches me that power is all that counts. I will respond more readily to being led.

9. Don't be inconsistent. That confuses me and makes me try harder to get away with everything that I can.

10. Don't make promises you are not going to keep. That will discourage my trust in you.

11. Don't let my "bad habits" get a lot of your attention. It may encourage me to continue them.

12. Don't try to discuss my behavior when I'm upset. For some reason, my hearing is not very good at that time.

13. Don't protect me from consequences. I need to learn from my own experiences.

14. Don't put me off when I ask questions. If you do, you will find that I stop asking.

15. Don't let my fears arouse your anxiety. Then I will become more afraid of failing.

Adults who see the importance of "connecting" with unmotivated children often use positive words of encouragement to communicate that they care. Try using phrases, such as the following, on a regular basis.

1. Can I help you?

2. What do you think?

3. I believe in you.

4. You're on the right track now!

5. That's the best you've ever done.

6. You're getting better every day.

7. Nothing can stop you now!

8. I knew you could do it!

9. I'm very proud of your hard work.

10. I'm happy to see you working like that.

11. Thanks for being responsible.

12. You've got your brain in gear today!

13. Well, look at you go!

14. I couldn't have done it better myself.

15. Now that's what I call a fine job.

16. That was first class work.

17. It's a pleasure to teach you when you work like that.

18. You really make my job fun.

19. You must have been practicing.

20. I know you will figure it out.

Strategy 79

20 Ways to Say Some Positive Words of Encouragement

Strategy 80

Increase Student Engagement

There are strategies that teachers can use to effectively engage most students in their classroom presentations. Below are 10 ideas that can increase participation.

1. In a jar, on separate pieces of paper, randomly pick out names and ask questions.

2. Give each student a laminated index card to hold up as a nonverbal response to each question. (agree on one side and disagree on other)

3. Set a kitchen timer giving a set number of minutes to complete an activity.

4. Have students pass a beanbag or nerfball™ to another student, who is to now answer the next question.

5. Use students' names often. Systematically make sure all students are included.

6. Have students use thumbs up for yes/true and thumbs down for no/false during class discussions.

7. Provide small individual chalkboards and chalk so students can write down their own answers.

8. Go down the roll book and call out names randomly.

9. Group students into fives. Ask questions to students, using the honor code, and record whether as a group they had the correct answer. The group with the most points gets 5 points added to their next test.

10. Systematically give positive feedback often.

What Are Your Students' Strongest Learning Styles?

Learning takes place when information is processed through our five basic senses.

1. Seeing—Visual Learner

2. Hearing—Auditory Learner

3. Touching—Tactile Learner

4. Feeling—Kinesthetic Learner

5. Tasting—Gustatory Learner

6. Smelling—Olfactory Learner

A learning style is a preferred way of thinking and understanding information. Adults need to put a lot of thought into lessons which encourage children to use their various learning senses. Variety and choice are the "key" when it comes to increased motivation. When planning a lesson ask yourself the following questions:

1. How many of the 5 basic senses are being challenged?

2. Can I implement an additional component to the lesson which is varied and exciting?

3. Do I need to provide an outline of the basic objectives?

4. Can I provide a tool for taking good notes?

Teachers who consider learning styles when they plan lessons will increase the probability that each student will experience success through his or her strongest learning style.

Strategy 82

Daily Class Rituals

There should always be time in every school day for teachers to energize and inspire their students to believe in themselves. One way to accomplish this is by using daily rituals. This is a time to "connect" with the class by sharing emotions, emphasizing good health, and staying abreast of events that create "teachable moments." Below are 10 examples of rituals which can be used as powerful classroom tools:

1. Greet students at the door with a smile, name, a handshake, or a high five.

2. Mind map the prior day's learning to review what the class accomplished and to guide today's schedule.

3. Have a stretching routine mid-morning to a favorite tune to make school more fun.

4. Have students write in a personal journal during the first 5 minutes of each day or period. Guarantee confidentiality and encourage them to be reflective in their writing. Check every 9 weeks that pages are written in and dated—but do not read what has been written.

5. Play music before certain activities. Use fun songs such as: " Rock Around the Clock," "La Bamba," "Great Balls of Fire," and "Pretty Woman."

6. Use positive affirmations each school day such as:

   • The more you learn the easier it gets!
   • The future belongs to those with serious dreams!
   • Inch by inch, it's a cinch!
   • Be bigger than your problems!

7. At the end of every day or class period, conclude by recognizing/recalling a student who has positively impressed the teacher through effort, compliance, questioning, humor, compassion, energy, etc. Keep a list to ensure that all receive recognition.

8. At the end of the day use a motivational cheer such as: "In your left hand put all your previous knowledge that you brought with you. In your right hand put all you have learned today. Now, when I say ready, Bring your hands together in a simple clap and say YES!

9. At the end of the day have students stand up, close their eyes, raise their shoulders, tighten fists, relax and listen as the teacher reviews the day's content.

10. Use a closing song to have students depart with a warm feeling. Songs like "Happy Trails", "Wonderful World", or "Getting Stronger" work well.

The teacher can set the tone for reducing test stress by communicating the fact that grades are not based solely on test scores. Class participation, mature attitudes, and leadership skills are also evaluated. (See the strategy: "E" for Effort on page 78)

Remind students that consistently taking good notes, reviewing assignments, and taking the time to quietly prepare for class are the keys to feeling calm when being tested.

During the test remember to:

breathe slowly

read directions twice

pace yourself and be aware of the time

eliminate the obvious wrong answers so you can make the best guess

always double check answers

Strategy 83
Reduce Test Stress

Teachers should review mistakes made on tests with the students. If possible, let students retake the test and average the two scores.

(Check out the "Test Buster" program available through Youth Light, Inc.)

Many students have few opportunities to think about and reflect upon their lives on a daily basis. Not only is such reflection helpful as a way of putting things into perspective, a daily reflection also enables students to verbally "write out" what has happened to them over the past 24 hours.

Requiring students to confidentially write for five minutes in a personal journal each day is a way to encourage reflection. You can use this as a five minute transition at the beginning of a class period (wonderful quiet time while you take attendance and get materials together to introduce a lesson) or during a particular time each day (e.g. after lunch). Have the students print the day and date at the top of each entry. Collect the diaries every six weeks to quickly scan the pages in class to affirm that every day has a written entry. Assure students that you will not read what they

Strategy 84
"Dear Diary" Learning to Reflect

wrote, you are only interested in validating that they made entries for each day.

Incidentally, because of this strategy, some students form a lifelong habit of writing daily in a personal journal and others keep their "school diary" well into adulthood as a cherished glimpse back into their childhood or adolescence.

Strategy 85

Professional Business Cards

Rarely do teachers take the time or bear the expense to order their own business cards. School districts should provide each teacher with 100 personal business cards each academic year or you can make your own personalized cards. The cards should give important information such as: name, school address and phone number, e-mail address, fax number, and the web site if available. By providing each parent with a personal business card, it communicates in a professional way that you are both interested in their student and accessible to them.

Strategy 86

Pen Pal Club!

Give your students a chance to meet new people and learn about other parts of the United States and other countries without leaving home. With a pen pal they can share information about themselves, their school and their neighborhood. They'll receive a list of pen pals to whom they can write. Sometimes by being more aware of places and peers around the world, students are able to look more objectively at themselves, their culture, their personal conduct, and their goals.

Students may write to:

International Pen Friends
Department FS6
1308 68th Lane North
Brooklyn Center, MN 55430   or

Locate electronic pen pals at such Web sites as:

www.epals.com
www. Classroomconnect.com

Responding To Your Pen Pal

Before each written response to a pen pal's letter, use prewriting activities. For example, have the students read their pen pal's letters aloud; quiz students about word and phrase meanings; paraphrase those words or phrases that are not understood; and have students highlight with their colored pens important words/phrases for use in their language activities. Use photographs from the pen pals' cultural group and exchange care packages with their pals. Have students underline questions in letters and encourage the class to come up with responses to those questions. Have the students type their revised letters into e-mails when possible.

Math is one subject area that often generates confusion, intimidation and fear in students. One math concept usually builds upon the next, so if students shy away from working hard to understand early math concepts, then they find themselves struggling with math throughout their school years.

Make Math Concrete and Fun!

It is important for teachers to present fun, but concrete, strategies to understand basic concepts. Below are a few basic ideas:

1. Use simple charts or number lines to provide concrete models which will help students get off to a good start when learning multiplication and place value. For example:

	1	2	3	4	5	6	7	8	9	10	11	12
6	6	12	18	24	30	36	42	48	54	60	66	72

thousand	hundred	ten	one	tenth	hundredth
1000	100	10	1	.1	.01

$6279.14 =$ 6   2   7   9 . 1   4

2. Division makes more sense to students when they think in terms of 4 basic steps repeated over and over until the problem is solved.

— divide — multiply — subtract — bring down the next number
Repeat the four steps again and again until all numbers are used.

```
      1 4 2  r 1
  4 ) 5 6 9
      4
      1 6
      1 6
          9
          8
          1
```

3. A few fun games always make math more fun and helps students see how math concepts are relevant to everyday life.

A. Line'em Up!

Ask the students what an item costs. (Show a picture from a magazine, ex.-car)
Put a price on a folded piece of paper. (for ex.- $18,498.00)
Put needed place value lines on the board and let the students write down their guess.
Unfold the listed price and talk about good approximations.

___ ___, ___ ___ ___. ___ ___

B. Higher or Lower!

Show a picture of an item. (for ex. mixer for $45.00)
Call on a student to guess the price. The only hint given is to say "higher or lower."
The student tries to name the correct price within 60 seconds.

Strategy 88

Using Manipulatives to Improve Handwriting Skills In Young Children

A student who can write well often has improved confidence, an increased concentration on content, and ultimately an improved academic performance. Students with poor handwriting skills often struggle with pen and paper tasks and are likely to become discouraged with lengthy writing assignments.

Handwriting skills begin during infancy. When babies reach, grasp, point, and release they strengthen their hand muscles. The more proficient the hand movements become, the more refined they also become, as the toddlers grow up and become ready for school.

There are numerous manipulation tasks that can be practiced to enable the child to successfully participate in classroom activities. Below are 10 ideas to consider including in elementary classes to facilitate hand muscle development.

1. Wringing out sponges and cleaning desks and blackboards
2. Punching holes and stapling paper
3. Lining up dominoes on their narrow end
4. Picking up delicate items, such as beans, with tweezers
5. Pinching labeled clothespins to match letters, numbers, or pictures
6. Cupping hands to shake and roll dice
7. Crumpling and throwing away trash
8. Opening and closing jars of many sizes
9. Forming letters using pipe cleaners
10. Using the tripod grasp, fade students from using thick chalk, pens or markers to smaller writing tools

When children begin handwriting they begin with a "static tripod grasp." With this grasp their writing tool is held with the thumb, index and middle fingers while the hand moves as a unit. The ring and little fingers do not provide stability for precise motions. The wrist mainly controls the writing movements. At the next level the children use the "dynamic tripod grasp." The thumb now works in opposition to the tip of the index finger. The ring and little fingers are flexed for stability. This grasp provides for maximum speed and refinement when writing. Make sure adults provide numerous manipulation tasks in order for strength to increase in the hand muscles. As a child's hand muscles strengthen, he/she will be less likely to become discouraged with assigned writing tasks. (One helpful tool to use in order to practice the "static tripod grasp" is the ball of a turkey baster. Children not only can squeeze it to increase muscle strength, but thick chalk can be inserted into the hole and prewriting skills can be practiced.)

General Classroom Accommodation:

1. Teach handwriting directly in a highly structured lesson of no longer than 15 minutes.
2. Use clear, consistent language to describe the formation of the strokes.
3. Insist on good posture.
4. Make sure that the paper is positioned at 20-35 degrees to the left for right-handers and 30-35 degrees to the right for left-handers.
5. Display models of good handwriting.
6. Set criteria for acceptable work, returning unacceptable work and providing positive, encouraging feedback.

Section 5

Parents' Strategies

Strategy 89

10 Things Parents Can Do To Help Children Develop A Healthy Self-Esteem

1. *Set and communicate high expectations.*

2. *Give caring and insightful feedback.*

3. *Encourage children to be involved in at least one school/community group.*

4. *Help children highly achieve in something they choose.*

5. *Set up opportunities for children to give of themselves to others.*

6. *Practice good decision making skills and independent work habits. (monitor TV, music, and computer time)*

7. *Establish a personal faith and respect in something greater then oneself.*

8. *Provide a warm, inviting atmosphere.*

9. *Aggressive behavior is not considered acceptable. Watch using sarcasm and negativism.*

10. *Monitor children's whereabouts!*

Strategy 90

What Should Parents Do to Help Decrease Bullying?

1. *Listen, ask, and talk about your child's school day.*

2. *Watch for any changes in behavior that concerns you.*

3. *Reduce or eliminate the amount of television time that involves violence.*

4. *Clearly communicate to your child that your family does not tolerate behavior that hurts another person.*

5. *Try avoiding physical punishment in your family. Set clear rules and follow through with consequences such as limiting privileges or using time out.*

6. *Expect your child's school to have written school rules regarding bullying. Consider serving on a parent committee.*

7. *Keep a written record of your observations concerning your child's behavior. Let the school know immediately if you believe your child has been bullied.*

8. *Teach and practice specific sentences with your child that can help him/her respond assertively to a bully. For example:*

    "Why are you acting childish?"

    "I don't have a problem, do you?"

Check out several books available through Youth Light on the topic of bullying: "Getting Equipped to Stop Bullying," "Eliminating Bullying" & others.

Strategy 91

Take Your Child With You To Work

Children often, and understandably, see their parent(s) or guardian(s) one dimensionally. They see mom or dad almost entirely in their parental role—usually at home.

Break the mold and let them see you, and them, in a different light. Fathers, take your daughters out to dinner for a one-on-one "date" once a month to really talk to each other and enjoy a different setting. Mothers, take your sons to a sporting event of their choice and ask them to explain the rules of the game to you.

Mothers and daughters and fathers and sons should take advantage of the annual "take your son/daughter to work" programs that are supported by many corporations and institutions. Ask your child to help both of you choose a new hobby, craft, sport, or skill that you can learn together.

Give your child a chance to see you as a multi-dimensional adult who isn't always in control, or totally competent, or constrained by the requirement to dole out rewards and punishments. Sometimes, just a significantly different setting can work miracles for the complex and powerful relationship between adult and child.

There is an old legend about the merits of fishing that says, "God adds another day to our lives for every day we go fishing; but he adds two days for every day we take a child fishing."

You may not add days to your life (although, there's that possibility), when you think creatively about taking your child with you to new settings and shared experiences; but you will almost certainly add joy, insights, and intimacy to your life!!

It is very easy for a parent to make sarcastic remarks to a child who is being disrespectful, sarcastic, or rebellious. However, please avoid the temptation to use sarcastic, verbal "put-downs." If not, parents are making two major mistakes: they are negatively role modeling to their children how to handle anger; and they are needlessly getting themselves upset.

By setting up fair rules, and following up with consistent rewards or punishments, there should be no need for a power struggle. It is important to hold your stinging tongue, even if you need to go into your bedroom and lock the door.

Children interpret offhand remarks as a sign of rejection. Underachievers often feel they are not living up to the

Strategy 92
Hold Your Tongue!

expectations of their parents so why try. The cost to a child's self esteem is just too great! The suggestion we give to children to "count to 10" before saying something you might regret holds true for parents as well. Hold your tongue and think through how to turn sarcasm and anger into hope and respect.

There will be times when parents would like more insight as to how their child is performing and interacting in school. Teachers can use videotaping to involve parents in monitoring school objectives and to increase parent awareness of their child's activities at school. It is always interesting to see how differently, for better or worse, students behave without parents being present. Parents may observe more independence and increased initiative from their child than they see at home. Teachers reported that parents had a better understanding of what they were discussing at parent-teacher conferences. Parents who are seldom able to come into school were able to see their child participating in a variety of activities.

Parents who choose to have a videotape of their child at school should receive a tape to view and return at

Strategy 93
Video Taping Students— Parents As Partners

least twice a school year. In addition to noting progress, the videotapes helped parents to identify difficulty on specific tasks. Videotapes can also be especially beneficial in providing feedback for Non-English speaking parents.

Strategy 94

Homework Checklist for Parents

Directions for Homework Checklist for Parents:

1. Fill in the dates for a nine-week grading period down the left column.

2. Decide on Sunday evening what reward the student will be working to earn during the upcoming week. Share ideas for this reward with the student.

3. Give one point for each 30 minutes spent on homework each day.

4. Total the points earned for the week on Thursday night.

5. Give rewards or privileges for seven or more points earned per week

It is a common belief that students who spend one hour per day doing homework usually pass their courses. Sometimes parents need to monitor and reward daily effort. Try using the homework checklist for parents that follows for a nine-week grading period and see if it makes a difference.

Homework/Study Time

Week	Monday	Tuesday	Wednesday	Thursday	Total
1					
2					
3					
4					
5					
6					
7					
8					
9					

Most children really want to get to know their parents better. Because adults lead such busy, stressful lives, other priorities take precedence and communication does not occur unless there is a problem or emergency. Under these circumstances the emotional theme is usually anger, fear or worry.

One good way to share time together that is positive is to share stories about personal experiences growing up. Share the fact that all adults have made mistakes or made poor choices and that most of the time learning took place. Children realize that parents do not expect perfection but that they do expect continual growth and effort to improve.

Strategy 95

Sharing Childhood Stories

Children, deep down, want to please their parents. By using childhood stories on a regular basis, children will get to know their parents better and together there will hopefully be a positive bonding experience that benefits all parties.

Strategy 96

Be Knowledgeable of Community Agencies

Parents often feel anxious about what they should be expecting academically and emotionally from an underachieving child. There are community agencies in most towns that work with children and their families, because some problems that children have are beyond the ability or authority of the school. (abuse, neglect, poverty, high or low unrealistic expectations, lack of consistent discipline, lack of stability)

Parents and educators should request intervention and assistance from community agencies if it is needed. Make sure schools maintain a close relationship with the local agencies that can share manpower and resources.

For example:
Department of Social Services;
Department of Youth Services;
Department of Juvenile Justice;
private counseling;
Big Brother/Big Sister;
speech or hearing therapists;
scouts; and
YMCA.

Strategy 97

Effective Communication with Parents

Even when teachers are frustrated with unmotivated students, whose parents may appear to be uninterested, it is most important to regularly exert the effort to communicate with their parents. Below are a few suggestions of ways to "open up" the lines of communication. Make sure the major theme of each contact is both positive and caring. Most parents will respond favorably when they witness teachers taking the time and displaying the effort to believe in their child's achievement.

- Make home visits, which provide invaluable insight.
- Make regular positive phone calls.
- Mail regular positive notes.
- E-Mail
- Fax
- Utilize self-monitoring tools which require a parent signature.

Strategy 98

Parent Club Meetings

Parents of underachievers can benefit from opportunities to problem solve with other parents in how to work with their children more effectively. Parents find comfort in realizing that there are other parents who have similar problems with their children.

By setting up a partnership between parents and the teacher to meet once a month, many positive outcomes can be expected. The monthly meeting could provide parents with ideas to:

- become more informed of school activities;
- consider different ways to handle discipline issues at home;
- discuss organizational techniques which could benefit the entire family;
- increase parents' high/low, but realistic, expectations of their child; and
- increase parents' positive attitudes toward their children and toward the school system.

Most students spend very little time talking and thinking about their future. Unmotivated underachievers probably spend even less time. Children today are part of the "instant gratification" culture. If achievements can not happen almost immediately, then they are not worth the effort.

When adults and students can have some private time to talk about the future, this can often be the catalyst to set realistic goals. (academic, social, & athletics) This time allows adults and students to really get to know each other and hopefully make a positive "connection." Students who believe their teachers and parents understand them, accept them, and like them are more likely to try harder and be respectful.

Strategy 99
Discussing the Future!

Strategy 100
Rules of the Road!

Sometimes parents don't take advantage of golden opportunities to communicate and connect with their children. Children want their parents to be interested in their lives, whether it is about family, friends or school. What better way to have some quality talk time then when you are driving in a car? Below are some rules to consider enforcing which could strengthen relationships.

1. Turn off all cell phones, CD players, and gameboys when riding in a car.

2. Be a good listener. Ask about your child's day but don't ask too many questions. Silence is OK too!!

3. Tune in to their music on the car radio. Who knows? Maybe you'll enjoy it too!

4. While driving, point out things of interest. It might be just the starter your child needs to tell or ask you something.

5. Pass around the day planner at "pick up" time so children write down after-school commitments and everyone is on the same schedule.

Strategy 101

Get the Lay of the Land!

Adults who want children to tell you more about a situation can be asked to draw a map of where kids sit in the cafeteria, who sits near them on a bus, what activities are occurring on the playground, etc. After drawing a map encourage the child to talk about the social situation at school and pay attention to all of the key players in this real-life soap opera. And like a soap opera, the adult should expect to go through several episodes before anything gets resolved. This strategy allows the child to design a map and discuss situations at the same time.

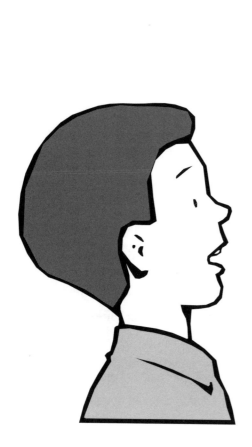

Amrein,A. (2003). *The effects of high-stakes testing on student motivation.* Educational Leadership, vol. 60, p.32.

Baumeister, R.F.& Leary, M.R. (1995). *The need to belong: Desire for interpersonal attachments as a fundamental human motivation.* Psychological Bulletin, 117, pp. 497-529.

Boatwright,B., Mathis,T. & Smith-Rex,S. (1998). *Getting equipped to stop bullying: A kid's survival kit for understanding and coping with violence in the schools.* Minneapolis,MN: Educational Media.

Coil, C. (2001). *220 strategies for success.* Marion,IL: Pieces of Learning.

Carr, T. (2000). *Children with anger problems.* Chapin, SC: :YouthLight.

Castillo,S., Mathis,T. & Smith-Rex,S. (1998). *Getting face to face with your fears: A kid's guide to understanding and coping with fears and phobias.* Minneapolis,MN: Educational Media.

Cell Phone Homework Hotline, USA Today, April 24, 2000.

Covington,M.V. (1992). *Making the grade: A self-worth perspective on motivation and school reform.* New York:Cambridge University Press

References

Garbarino,J. (1995). *Lost boys*. New York: Free Press.

Francis, L. (1992). *Primary school size and pupil attitudes: Small is happy?* Educational Management and Administration, vol.20, pp. 100-104.

Frank,T. & Smith-Rex,S. (2001). *ADHD: 102 practical strategies for "reducing the deficit."* Chapin,SC: YouthLight.

Frank,T. & Smith-Rex,S. (1995). *Getting a life of your own: A kid's guide to understanding and coping with family alcoholism.* Minneapolis, MN: Educational Media.

Frank,T. & Smith-Rex,S. (1996). *Getting over the blues: A kid's guide to understanding and coping with unpleasant feelings and depression.* Minneapolis,MN: Educational Media.

Frank,T. & Smith-Rex,S. (1997). *Getting with it: A kid's guide to forming good relationships and "fitting in."* Minneapolis,MN: Educational Media.

Goodman,J. (1995). *Laffirmations: 1001 ways to add humor to your life and work.* Deerfield Beach, FL: Health Communications, Inc.

Harter,S. (1996). *Teacher and classmate influences on scholastic motivation self-esteem, and level of voice in adolescents.* New York: Cambridge.

Harvey,V. (1991). *Children and perfectionism. Parent/Teacher Handout.* National Association of School Psychologists.

Holloway,J. (2002). *Extracurricular activities and student motivation.* Educational Leadership, vol. 60, p. 80.

Mathis,T. & Smith-Rex,S. (2001). *Getting ahead: Strategies to motivate and assist students with classroom learning.* Minneapolis,MN: Educational Media.

Mueller,C., Dweck,C. (December, 1998). *The right kind of praise.* Family Therapy Network, 601-611.

Noddings,N. (1992). *The challenge to care in schools: An alternative approach to education.* New York: Teachers College Press.

Parker,J.G. & Asher,S.R. (1987). *Peer relations and later personal adjustment: Are low-accepted kids at risk?* Psychology Bulletin, 102, 357-389.

Raffini,J. (1996). *150 ways to increase intrinsic motivation in the classroom.* Needham Heights, Mass: Simon & Schuster.

Pairi,S. (2001). *Loneliness in children with disabilities.* Teaching Exceptional Children, vol. 33, pp. 52-58.

Sears,S.J. & Millburn,J. (1990). *School-age stress. Childhood Stress,* edited by Arnold,E., New York: John Wiley and Sons.

Shapiro,L. (1994). *Tricks of the trade.* King of Prussia, Pa: Center for Applied Psychology, Inc.

St. Michel,C. (2004). *Is your child a quitter?* Good Housekeeping, Feb.

Tavris,C. (1984). *On the wisdom of counting to ten.* Review of Personality & Social Psychology, 170-191. New York: P. Shaver, Sage.

Weiner,B. (1992). *Human motivation. Metaphors, theories, and research.* Newbury Park, CA: Sage.

Wentzel,K. (1997). *Student motivation in middle school: the role of perceived pedagogical caring.* Journal of Educational Psychology, Vol.89 (3) pp. 411-419.

Woodard,J. (Nov.,1998). *A personal encounter with the power of story telling.* Educational Week, 27.